对外汉语本科系列教材
语言技能类（二年级）

英 汉 翻 译 教 程

杜玉兰　主编
熊文华　编著

北京语言大学出版社
BEIJING LANGUAGE AND CULTURE
UNIVERSITY PRESS

©2001 北京语言大学出版社，社图号 01058

图书在版编目（CIP）数据

英汉翻译教程 二年级 ／ 杜玉兰主编：熊文华编著 .
-- 北京 ： 北京语言大学出版社，2001.7（2018.9 重印）
ISBN 978-7-5619-0955-3

Ⅰ．①英… Ⅱ．①杜… ②熊… Ⅲ．①汉语－翻译－
对外汉语教学－教材 Ⅳ．①H195.4

中国版本图书馆 CIP 数据核字(2001)第 036594 号

英汉翻译教程 二年级
YING-HAN FANYI JIAOCHENG （ER NIANJI）

责任编辑： 梁 骁 张 建
责任印制： 周 燚

出版发行： 北京语言大学出版社
社　　址： 北京市海淀区学院路 15 号，100083
网　　址： www.blcup.com
电子信箱： service@blcup.com
电　　话： 编 辑 部　8610-82303647/3592/3395
　　　　　　国内发行　8610-82303650/3591/3648
　　　　　　海外发行　8610-82303365/3080/3668
　　　　　　北语书店　8610-82303653
　　　　　　网购咨询　8610-82303908
印　　刷： 北京虎彩文化传播有限公司

版　次： 2001 年 7 月第 1 版　　　**印　次：** 2018 年 9 月第 6 次印刷
开　本： 787 毫米×1092 毫米 1/16　**印　张：** 8.25
字　数： 114 千字
定　价： 29.00 元

PRINTED IN CHINA

序

李　杨

　　教材是教育思想和教学原则、要求、方法的物化,是教师将知识传授给学生,培养学生能力的重要中介物。它不仅是学生学习的依据,也体现了对教师进行教学工作的基本规范。一部优秀的教材往往凝结着几代人的教学经验及理论探索。认真编写教材,不断创新,一直是我们北京语言大学的一项重点工作。对外汉语本科教育,从 1975 年在北京语言学院(北京语言大学的前身)试办现代汉语专业(今汉语言专业)算起,走过了二十多年行程。如今教学规模扩大,课程设置、学科建设都有了明显发展。在总体设计下,编一套包括四个年级几十门课程的系列教材的条件业已成熟。进入 90 年代,我们开始了这套教材的基本建设。

　　北京语言大学留学生本科教育,分为汉语言专业(包括该专业的经贸方向)和中国语言文化专业。教学总目标是培养留学生熟练运用汉语的能力,具备扎实的汉语基础知识、一定的专业理论与基本的中国人文知识,造就熟悉中国国情文化背景的应用型汉语人才。为了实现这个目标,学生从汉语零起点开始到大学毕业,要经过四年八个学期近 3000 学时的学习,要修几十门课程。这些课程大体上分为语言课,即汉语言技能(语言能力、语言交际能力)课、汉语言知识课,以及其他中国人文知识课(另外适当开设体育课、计算机课、第二外语课)。为留学生开设的汉语课属于第二语言教学性质,它在整个课程体系中处于核心地位。教学经验证明,专项技能训练容易使某个方面的能力迅速得到强化;而由于语言运用的多样性、综合性的要求,必须进行综合性的训练才能培养具有实际意义的语言能力。因此在语言技能课中,我们走的是综合课与专项技能课相结合的路子。作为必修课的综合课从一年级开到四年级。专项技能课每学年均分别开设,并注意衔接和加深。同时,根据汉语基本要素及应用规律,系统开设汉语言本体理论知识课程。根据中国其他人文学科如政治、经济、历史、文化、文学、哲学等基础知识,从基本要求出发,逐步开设文化理论知识课程。专业及专业方向从三年级开始划分。其课程体系大致是:

一年级

　　汉语综合课:初级汉语
　　汉语专项技能课:听力课、读写课、口语课、视听课、写作课

二年级

　　汉　语　综　合　课：中级汉语

　　汉语专项技能课：听力口语、阅读、写作、翻译、报刊语言基础、新闻听
　　　　　　　　　　力

　　汉　语　知　识　课：现代汉语语音、汉字

　　文　化　知　识　课：中国地理、中国近现代史

三年级

　　汉　语　综　合　课：高级汉语（汉语言专业）
　　　　　　　　　　中国社会概览（中国语言文化专业）

　　汉语专项技能课：高级口语、写作、翻译、报刊阅读、古代汉语；经贸口
　　　　　　　　　　语、经贸写作（经贸方向）

　　汉　语　知　识　课：现代汉语词汇

　　文　化　知　识　课：中国文化史、中国哲学史、中国古代史、中国现代文
　　　　　　　　　　学史；中国国情、中国民俗、中国艺术史（中国语言文
　　　　　　　　　　化专业）；当代中国经济（经贸方向）

四年级

　　汉　语　综　合　课：高级汉语（汉语言专业）
　　　　　　　　　　中国社会概览（中国语言文化专业）

　　汉语专项技能课：当代中国话题、汉语古籍选读、翻译；
　　　　　　　　　　高级商贸口语（经贸方向）

　　汉　语　知　识　课：现代汉语语法、修辞

　　文　化　知　识　课：中国古代文学史；中国对外经济贸易、中国涉外经济
　　　　　　　　　　法规（经贸方向）；儒道佛研究、中国戏曲、中国古代
　　　　　　　　　　小说史、中外文化交流（中国语言文化专业）

　　这套总数为50余部的系列教材完全是为上述课程设置而配备的，除两部高级汉语教材是由原教材修订并入本系列外，绝大部分都是新编写的。

　　这是一套跨世纪的新教材，它的真正价值属于21世纪。其特点是：

　　1. 系统性强。对外汉语本科专业、年级、课程、教材之间是一个具有严密科学性的系统，如图（见下页）：

　　整套教材是在系统教学设计的指导下完成的，每部教材都有其准确的定性与定位。除了学院和系总体设计之外，为子系统目标的实现，一年级的汉语教科书（10部）和二、三、四年级的中国文化教科书（18部）均设有专门的专家编委会，负责制定本系列教材的编写原则、方法，并为每一部教材的质量负责。

　　2. 有新意。一部教材是否有新意、有突破，关键在于它对本学科理论和本课程教学有无深入的甚至是独到的见解。这次编写的整套教材，对几个大的子

系列和每一部教材都进行了反复论证。从教学实际出发,对原有教材的优点和缺点从理论上进行总结分析,根据国内外语言学、语言教学和语言习得理论以及中国文化诸学科研究的新成果,提出新思路,制定新框架。这样就使每一个子系列内部的所有编写者在知识与能力、语言与文化、实用性与学术性等主要问题上取得共识。重新编写的几十部教材,均有所进步,其中不少已成为具有换代意义的新教材。

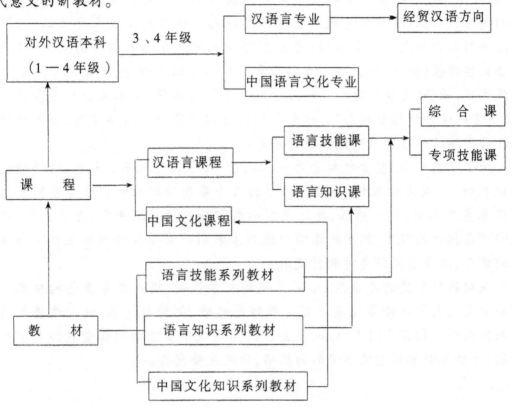

3. 有明确的量化标准。在这套教材编写前和进行过程中,初、中、高对外汉语教学的语音、词汇、语法、功能、测试大纲及语言技能等级标准陆续编成,如《中高级对外汉语教学等级大纲》(1995 年,孙瑞珍等)、《初级对外汉语教学等级大纲》(1997 年,杨寄洲等)。一年级全部教材都是在这些大纲的监控下编写的,二、三、四年级汉语教材也都自觉接受大纲的约束,在编写过程中不断以大纲检查所使用的语料是否符合标准,是否在合理的浮动范围内。中国文化教材中的词汇也参照大纲进行控制,语言难度基本上和本年级汉语教材相当,使学生能够在略查辞典的情况下自学。这样就使这套教材在科学性上前进了一步。

4. 生动性与学术性相结合。本科留学生是成年人,至少具有高中毕业的文化水平,他们所不懂的仅仅是作为外语的汉语而已。因此教材必须适合成年人的需要并具有相当的文化品位。我们在编写各种汉语教材时,尽可能采用那些能反映当代中国社会和中国人的生活、心态的语料和文章,使学生能够及时了解中国社会生活及其发展变化，学到鲜活的语言。一些入选的经典作品也在编排练习时注意着重学习那些至今依然富有生命力的语言，使教材生动、有趣味、有相对的稳定性。教材的学术性一方面表现为教材内容的准确和编排设计的科学，更重要的是，课程本身应当能够及时反映出本学科的新水平和新进展。这些都成为整套教材编写的基本要求之一。文化类教材，编写之初编委会就提出，要坚持"基础性（主要进行有关学科的基础知识和基本理论教育，不追求内容的高深）、共识性（内容与观点在学术界得到公认或大多数人有共识，一般不介绍个别学者的看法）、全貌性（比较完整与系统地介绍本学科面貌，可以多编少讲）、实用性（便于学生学习，有利于掌握基本知识与理论，并有助于汉语水平的提高）"，强调"要能反映本学科的学术水平"，要求将"学术品位和内容的基础性、语言的通俗性结合起来"。作者在编写过程中遵循了这些原则，每部教材都能在共同描绘的蓝图里创造独特的光彩。

为了方便起见，整套教材分为一、二、三、四年级汉语语言教材、汉语理论与知识教材、中国文化教材、经贸汉语教材五个系列陆续出版。这套系列教材由于课程覆盖面大，层次感强，其他类型的教学如汉语短期教学、进修教学、预备教学可在相近的程度、相同的课型中选用本教材。自学汉语的学生亦可根据自己的需要，选择不同门类的教材使用。

教材的科学更新与发展，是不断强化教学机制、提高教学质量的根本。北京语言文化大学汉语学院集近百位教师的经验、智慧与汗水，编就这套新的大型系列教材。相信它问世以后，将会在教学实践中多方面地接受教师与学生的检验，并会不断地融进使用者的新思路，使之更臻完善。

编者的话

使用对象

《英汉翻译教程》是为学习现代汉语专业的外国留学生编写的一套教材。本教材分为三册,分别供二、三、四年级教学使用。

课型性质

英汉翻译课是一门语言技能训练课。这门课的教学目的与其他汉语课型既有共同之处,亦有不同之处。共同之处是旨在提高学生的汉语综合运用能力;不同之处是旨在突出英汉两种语言和文化的对比,让学生了解二者的差异,通过英汉翻译训练,使学生能够跨越语言与文化障碍,达到交际的目的。为此,就要讲授翻译的理论与技巧,并以独特的双语教学手段授课。把握住这一点则定能体现出这门课的独特教学功能。

编写原则

以学生课上的翻译实践为主,在此基础上加以归纳总结并上升到翻译理论。以英语译为汉语为主,紧紧围绕学生学习汉语的这一主攻方向,辅以汉译英的练习。为在课上和课下充分发挥学生学习的主动性,提高教学效果,我们没有提供课文译文及练习答案。

编写体例

课文　选材范围广泛,文化气息浓厚,让学生接触到各个方面的内容,既学习翻译知识,又了解社会文化。四年级教材课文内容带有一定的专题性质,故选材起点放低,易于熟巧教学程序的推进。四年级教材还有五课备用课文供教师选择使用。

注释　二、三年级教材给出专有名词及部分难词、难句的汉语翻译;四年级只给出部分专有名词的汉语翻译。所给出的注释以逐册减少为原则。

译词分析　二年级教材有部分译词分析和译法分析。三、四年级教材有译句分
译法分析　析。选择课文中的典型词,在某方面有代表性的句子或难句,在翻
译句分析　译方法及翻译思路上简明扼要地加以提示或分析。同一内容在各册中时有交叉,但分析的难易程度有所侧重,强调的角度有所不同,不断增加新意,使学生温故而知新,循环往复,收获便在其中。

翻译理论　　每册若干课之后，或一个单元之后都编有一课翻译理论或方法，将
与方法　　前面课文中反复练习实践的内容提升到理论的高度，实现由实践到
　　　　　理论的原则。将译句分析中"点"的分析扩展到"面"的论述，实现
　　　　　"点"、"面"结合的原则。

练习　　练习以英译汉为主。每课含有三至四个练习项目，包括译词、译法
　　　　或译句分析所涉及的内容及若干较为重要的应掌握的其他问题。练
　　　　习形式力求多样，从不同的角度达到巩固所学的内容的目的。

教学安排

二年级为初学起步阶段，每周二学时。

三年级为系统学习阶段，每周四学时。

四年级为提高熟巧程度阶段，每周四学时。

致谢

本教程所选用的文章选自国内外出版的英文报刊、书籍，国内英文报纸，以
《中国日报》为多。凡是能与这些文章的作者取得联系的，均已函告。有些文章
几经转载，出处不详，难以与作者取得联系。本教程尚有一些段落、句子引自其
他书籍、词典。在此，向原作者一并致谢。

祝愿

使用本教程的同学们，无论你将来从事翻译工作，还是从事与汉语有关的
其他工作，愿这套教程从你学习之日起即成为你的朋友，并送你踏上事业的成
功之路。

2000 年 8 月

CONTENTS 目录

Lesson 1
Meeting People

A: Good evening!

B: Good evening! Come in, please. Let me take your coat. How nice to see you again. Have you been away lately?[①]

A: Yes, I've been away on holiday.

B: Let's go into the sitting room. Now, what can I get you?

A: Tea, please.

B: Right you are. By the way, do you know Peter and Susan[②]?

A: No, but I'd like to meet them.

B: (Going to C and D) This is Riaz from Pakistan, and Susan from the United States, and Peter from England.

A: How do you do?

C and D: How do you do?

A: When did you start your Chinese course at the University?

C and D: Last October.

A: And how do you like Beijing?

C: It's quite different from what I thought.

D: Beijing is certainly a beautiful city. But if it wasn't for the cold winter, I'd like it very much.[③]

A: Don't worry, you'll get used to everything here in a year or two.

. . . .

C and D: ...Well, we really have enjoyed ourselves.[④] It was a delightful party, but it's time we were off.

B: Oh, dear! So soon? Can't you stay a little longer?

C: I'd love to, but I have to be up early tomorrow.

B: What a shame! Let's see where your coats are. Oh, over there. Can you find your way back all right?[⑤]

C: Yes, we'll take a taxi. Thank you for the wonderful meal.

B: I'm glad you enjoyed it. Good night!

C and D: Good night!

● 注　释 ●

① Have you been away lately?

你最近去外地了吧?（也可译为"你前些日子外出了吧?"或"……不在家吧?"）

② Peter　　彼得

Susan　　苏珊

Riaz　　里亚兹

③ if it wasn't for the cold winter, I'd like it very much.

要不是冬天这么冷,我还真喜欢这儿。

④ we really have enjoyed ourselves.

我们实在玩得很高兴。

⑤ Can you find your way back all right?

回去的路你们还找得着吗?

※ 译词分析 ※

"party"的翻译

一个多义项的英语词语,在不同的句子中可能有不同的翻译,这是容易理解的;但是单一义项的同一词语在不同的句子中,由于对应的汉语表达方式搭配不同,翻译也可能不同。这一点我们应该特别注意。英语"party"指"社交活动"时,根据不同的搭配有不同的译法。例如:

◇ a tea party　　茶会　　　　◇ a dancing party　　　舞会

◇ a dinner party　宴会　　　　◇ give a birthday party　过生日

◇ It was a lovely party.　　这次聚会很有意思。

练　习

1. 翻译对话:

A: How do you do?

B: How do you do? Pleased to meet you.

A: The pleasure is mine.

B: How do you find things over here?

A: Everything is new to me, and I'm still feeling pretty homesick.

B: It's bound to be strange at first, but it won't take you long to settle down here.

2

2. 翻译下列几组对话，注意"yes"和"no"的译法。

A：Will it take me long to get there?

B：No, it's no distance at all.

A：Is your driving license valid?

B：Yes, it doesn't expire till next January.

A：Do you mind if I open the window?

B：No, it's stuffy here.

A：We don't want to make any mistake, do we?

B：No, we don't.

A：Isn't it out of your way if you give me a lift?

B：No, it's on my way home.

A：Are you sure it's not too much trouble for you to do so?

B：Yes, I am.

A：Is there nothing else to be done?

B：No, nothing.

3. 下面句子中画横线的词都有四个汉语译词。选择其中最恰当的一个把全句译出。

（1）I'd like you to meet my brother Sam.

（A. 遇见　　B. 认识　　C. 碰上　　D. 碰到）

（2）What do you think of life there in London?

（A. 思念　　B. 想起　　C. 考虑　　D. 觉得）

（3）Hope you can come again.

（A. 又　　B. 再　　C. 还　　D. 另）

（4）Go right to the end of the street, and you can't miss it.

（A. 一直　　B. 正确　　C.右边　　D. 不错）

Lesson 2
Sports

A: Hello, Xiao Wang. We're going to the club this afternoon. Would you like to play a mixed doubles① with us?

B: No, I'm afraid not. It's not that I don't like playing with you, but I'm tired out. I played a match against Lao Zhang yesterday and I haven't got over it yet. My arms are still aching. So I'd rather leave it for another day.② I hope you don't mind me saying "no".

A: No, I don't. How did you get on in the match? Who won?

B: I did. I managed to beat him in the end. Unfortunately it started to rain half-way through the game and I couldn't stand playing in the rain. I suggested going on with the match later, but he disagreed, because he had arranged to go out with his friends.

A: So you finally defeated him?

B: Yes. I made him run about all the time.

A: Obviously if one wants to win a match one must get rid of all worries and be self-confident.③

B: That's true. By the way, would you like to go to the cinema with me next Sunday? There'll be a new film at the Wudaokou Cinema.

A: I'd love to. What's it about?

B: *Endless*④, a Chinese movie with English subtitles. It's supposed to be funny. When shall I call for you? At about nine?

A: Let's say ten o'clock, just to make sure I'm up.

B: Do you still find it a great trouble to get up at seven o'clock in the morning?

A: Except weekdays, yes.

● 注　　释 ●

① a mixed doubles
混合双打
② I'd rather leave it for another day.
我想不如改日再打。

4

③ one must get rid of all worries and be self-confident.

你得消除烦恼,充满自信。

④ *Endless*

《没完没了》

※ 译词分析 ※

"play"的翻译

英语动词"play"在不同的短语中翻译有所不同。例如:

◇ The children are playing in the garden.

孩子们在花园中玩。

◇ play a mixed doubles

参加混合双打

◇ play the guitar

弹吉他

◇ play football

踢足球

◇ play the flute

吹笛子

◇ play him at chess

跟他下棋

============= 练　　习 =============

1. **翻译短文:**

A: What are the most popular sports in China today?

B: Well, there is football, basketball, volleyball, track and field sports.

A: What are the indoor games and sports?

B: Oh, there's table tennis, badminton, swimming, weightlifting, *wushu*, chess, billiards and so on.

A: Do you play hockey, golf and tennis?

B: Yes, we do. Tennis is played all the year round on hard or grass courts.

A: What about winter sports?

B: In the north, winter is the great time for skating and skiing.

2. 翻译下列句子，注意"**play**"的译法。

(1) Tell the children not to play out in the rain.

(2) The two teams played off seven games against each other.

(3) He likes playing the flute.

(4) Her seven-year-old sister wanted to learn how to play the piano.

(5) My muscles are sore from playing badminton.

(6) When you played football, what position did you play?

(7) Will you play me at chess?

3. 完成下列句子的翻译：

(1) Baseball is my favourite sport. What's your favourite?

我最喜欢打棒球。_____?

(2) We went fishing early this morning, but we didn't catch anything.

今天一早我们就去钓鱼，但是_____。

(3) My younger sister swam three miles in nine hours.

我妹妹在九小时_____。

(4) I like playing tennis in the summer. My favourite winter sport is skating.

夏天我喜欢打网球，_____。

Lesson 3
At the Barber's

A: And the next gentleman, please. How would you like it cut, sir?[①]

B: Oh, fairly short, please, but not too much off the top.

A: Are you over here on a visit, sir?

B: No. I'm a student. I've been learning Chinese at this university since 1998.

A: I see. No wonder you speak Chinese so well. Do you sometimes get home-sick?

B: Homesick? You mean... do I ever wish I were back home? Never! I wouldn't go back before I complete my M.A. course.

A: But life would be easier if you lived at home.

B: My wife is here with me.

A: Oh, is she? ...Is that enough off the top?

B: Yes, that'll do fine. But can you please take a little more off the sides, I wonder?

A: Certainly, sir.

B: Oh, and I think I might as well have a shampoo while I'm at it.[②]

A: Very good. Any particular kind?

B: No, I'll leave that to you.

A: Shall I put some oil on?

B: No, I don't think so. Oily hair makes a student like me look funny[③], you know....How much is that?

A: Ten *yuan*, sir.

B: Here you are.

A: Thank you very much. Good-bye! And the next gentleman, please.

● 注　释 ●

① How would you like it cut, sir?
先生,您想怎么理?

② I think I might as well have a shampoo while I'm at it.
我想还是顺便洗个头吧。

③ Oily hair makes a student ... look funny.

……学生头发油光锃亮的看起来有点滑稽可笑。

※ 译词分析 ※

"next"的翻译

英语"next"的意义比较单一,但是把它译成汉语时由于搭配不同,选词也有所不同。例如:

◇ next gentleman　　　　下一位(先生)
◇ next year　　　　　　明年
◇ the next two pages　　后面两页
◇ next-door neighbour　隔壁邻居

※ 译法分析 ※

否定句的焦点位移

英语的否定句译成汉语时其否定词的位置一般与原来的相同,但是由于表达方式的差异,译文也可能出现否定焦点位移的情况。所谓"否定焦点"就是指被否定的主要内容(信息中心),在对话中则指答话人所否定的疑点。例如:

A: Would you like to play a mixed doubles with us?
　　我们来个混合双打怎么样?

B: No, I'm afraid not. It's not that I don't like playing with you, but I'm tired out.
　　不,恐怕不行。不是我不愿意跟你们打,是因为我太累了。

A: Shall I put some oil on?
　　要使发油吗?

B: No, I don't think so, thanks.
　　不,我想不必了,谢谢。

(如果把第四句译为"不,我不认为是这样",那就不符合汉语表达习惯了。)

A: I hope you don't mind me saying "no".
　　我说"不去",希望你别介意。(否定焦点一致,但语序有变化)

B: No, I don't.
　　噢,没什么。

(英语否定副词被汉译为语气词;"没什么"的隐含主语不是"我",而是"这"。)

◇ If it wasn't for the cold winter, I'd like it very much.

要是冬天不这么冷,我还真喜欢这儿。

(英语"not"用于对"was"的否定,但是在对译的汉语句子中"不"用于否定"这么冷"。)

 练　　习

1．翻译对话:

A：Good afternoon, sir. What can I do for you?

B：Haircut and shave, please.

A：Take a seat, please. I'll be with you in a minute. . . . Now do you want it cut short or just trimmed?

B：Not too short, I think.

A：Your hair seems rather dry. A shampoo will do it a lot of good.

B：Then I'll have a shampoo.

A：And now for the shave. I must say your skin's rather tender, but you needn't worry. I've never cut any customer, you know.

B：And now, how much do I owe you?

A：That'll be nine *yuan* altogether.

2．把下列句子译成汉语,注意"next"的译法。

(1) Take the next turning to the right and go straight on.

(2) Which is the city next to Beijing in size?

(3) There are no tickets left for today's show. The next best thing is to visit the Summer Palace.

(4) She will spend the first week of her holiday in Shanghai and the next in Guangzhou.

(5) That winter was very cold; and the next winter was even colder.

(6) Next to pop music, pingpong was his greatest love.

(7) When I next saw her she was wearing a troubled look.

3．从所给词语中选择一个恰当的翻译下列句子:

(1) Do you want me to <u>shampoo</u> your hair?

(香波,洗发水,洗)

(2) Could you <u>take</u> a little more off the top, please?

(剪去,拿走,理发)

(3) Mrs. Zhang is going to the hairdresser's to have her hair <u>done</u>.
  (做,作,理)

(4) My brother likes the way the barber <u>cuts</u> his hair.
  (切,割,理)

(5) I asked the barber not to give me a short haircut, but my Chinese <u>failed me</u>.
  (失败了我,没有把意思说清楚,不及格)

Lesson 4
Weather

A: Was it very cold last winter?

B: Yes, it was. All the ponds, lakes and rivers were frozen over, and the roads were covered with slippery ice or deep snow. Bitter north winds stripped all trees of their leaves.①

A: You're talking about last winter in Beijing, aren't you? But China is so vast, are there any climatic differences in various parts of the country?

B: Yes. There's a difference of more than 33℃ in winter temperatures between Guangzhou in the south and Harbin in the north. Generally speaking, some provinces have a longer winter and practically no summer, others are warm all the year round and have no real winter.②

A: What's summer like in Beijing? Is it always as hot as in New Delhi③?

B: No, I don't think so. July can be very hot, but it's always cool in the morning and evening; and if the heat wave lasts too long, black clouds sometimes cover the sky all of a sudden.④ After a heavy fall of rain, everything looks fresh and bright again.

A: What's the best season in Beijing: spring or autumn?

B: Well, I think autumn is marvelous. It's sunny and warm, and the sky is blue and cloudless. In late October the woods begin to turn yellow and brown, and the paths are covered with fallen leaves. It's beautiful!

A: What about spring? Is it very windy?

B: February and March are cold and windy, but gradually the weather gets milder and the snow begins to melt.⑤ It's the season farmers do their ploughing.

● 注　释 ●

① Bitter north winds stripped all trees of their leaves.
寒冷的北风刮落了所有的树叶。

② others are warm all the year round and have no real winter.
其他省份一年四季都很暖和,没有真正的冬天。

11

③ New Delhi　　新德里

④ if the heat wave lasts too long, black clouds sometimes cover the sky all of a sudden.

要是热浪持续的时间太长,有时天空也会突然乌云密布。

⑤ but gradually the weather gets milder and the snow begins to melt.

不过天气逐渐暖和起来,雪也开始融化。

※ 译词分析 ※

译词的音节

汉语很讲究节奏。这除了表现在声调、重音、声母和韵母结合的和谐以及句式的对称外,还表现在句子或短语中一些音节的必要平衡。例如本课课文中的"ponds, lakes and rivers",既可以译为"塘、湖和河",又可以译为"池塘、湖泊和河流"。现代汉语中名词多为双音节,因此按照后一种译法念起来较为流畅。如果在这几个并列名词的翻译中混用单音节和多音节译词,就会失去音节上的平衡,念起来就不顺口。

同样地,在翻译本课的"slippery ice or deep snow","morning and evening","fresh and bright","spring or autumn","sunny and warm","blue and cloudless","yellow and brown"和"cold and windy"等词组时,也都应该注意译词结构上的一致和音节上的协调。

※ 译法分析 ※

以引导词"there"开头的英语句子与汉语的存现句

英语"there + verb/be"的句子常常可以用汉语的存现句来翻译。

英语"there + verb/be + noun + place/time"的句式与汉语的存现句结构近似,成分相同,因此常常以它为对等翻译句式。不同的地方是:这类英语叙述句开头的引导词本身没有具体意义,句子中的名词后面是地点或时间,而在汉语同类句子中这些状语一般都放在句首。请比较:

◇ There's a difference of more than 33℃ in winter temperatures between Guangzhou in the south and Harbin in the north.

在南方的广州与北方的哈尔滨冬季温差超过 33 摄氏度。

◇ There are climatic differences in various parts of the country.

全国各地气候不同。

翻译结构较复杂的这类长句时可以参考汉语存现句的结构,但是不一定每句都完全套用它。

══════ 练 习 ══════

1. 翻译短文:

In the city, the thunderstorm is a break in the weather, the climax of a heat wave and the forerunner of a cooler interval. In the suburbs, the thunderstorm cools things off, is good for the lawn and the fairways, and saves the flowers from midsummer scorching. In the country, it is a godsend after blistering heat that has curled the corn and parched the pastureland. It is a blessing, unless the farmer has 20 acres of hay in windrows, ready to bale tomorrow.

2. 翻译下面的句子,如果可能,采用汉语存现句句式。

(1) There is quite a big collection of books in our library.

(2) There aren't any good seats left for Saturday's evening show.

(3) There seems to be a large number of good restaurants in this town.

(4) When I was a child there were some people whose ideas I respected.

(5) There wasn't anything he didn't know about baseball.

(6) There are several different styles of shoes in your size.

3. 翻译下面的句子,注意结构和译词的音节平衡。

(1) At seven I got dressed, brushed my teeth, combed my hair and went downstairs for breakfast.

(2) He doesn't like to go to bed at night but he doesn't mind getting up in the early morning.

(3) Least talk, most work.

(4) Hope for the best, prepare for the worst.

(5) Summer is the farmer's busy season. The grass must be cut and the hay must be made while the dry weather lasts.

(6) In late autumn the days get shorter and the nights longer. The woods turn yellow and brown.

(7) Everybody talks about the weather, but nobody does anything about it.

Lesson 5
At the Supermarket

Until two years ago I hated supermarkets. An aunt of mine owned a small grocer's shop which was put out of business[①] when a supermarket opened nearby. She couldn't compete with prices, and in the end her customers preferred to save money rather than have her friendly, personal service. In order to build that supermarket they knocked down three fine eighteenth-century houses. It also meant the end of the Saturday street market in the area.[②]

Two years ago my firm transferred me to their Paris branch[③]. My spoken French was terrible and I was afraid to use it in shops. The local supermarket saved me. I was able to shop there without uttering a single word of French[④]. I came to enjoy wheeling my trolley round[⑤], inspecting the shelves stocked high with goods. And it was cheap, I discovered. I was converted.

A large supermarket can be a complex business. It is usually divided into the fruit and vegetable department, the meat department, the bakery department and the grocery department. Some supermarkets even have playrooms where mothers can leave their children while shopping. Now I belong to those customers who do their shopping at a supermarket at least once a week.

● 注　　释 ●

① was put out of business
生意就被挤垮了
② It also meant the end of the Saturday street market in the area.
这也意味着该地区星期六的街头集市就此结束。
③ their Paris branch
巴黎分公司
④ without uttering a single word of French
不讲一句法语
⑤ I came to enjoy wheeling my trolley round.
我渐渐地喜欢推着小车四下里转。

14

※ 译法分析 ※

同形异类词的翻译

在汉语和英语中都有许多词形(拼写)相同但是词类不一样的词,只有在具体句子中才能看出它的语法形态或功能的差别。这一类英语词往往可以用写法和意思不同的对等汉语词语进行翻译;反过来说,把这类汉语词语译成英语时情况也一样。请比较下面的句子:

◇ An aunt of mine owned a small grocer's shop.

我的一个婶婶开过一个小杂货铺。

◇ I was able to shop there without uttering a single word of French.

我到那儿买东西可以不讲一句法语。

◇ The front wheel of an old bicycle was rather larger than the one at the back.

老式的自行车前轮大后轮小。

◇ I came to enjoy wheeling my trolley round.

我渐渐地喜欢推着小车四下里转。

============ 练 习 ============

1.翻译短文:

Supermarkets aim to provide a housewife with all her needs under one roof. At the entrance she picks up a wire basket and, to the accompaniment of soft background music, she moves from counter to counter, from shelf to shelf, selecting her groceries, her meat, her vegetables, even sometimes her crockery or clothes, until her basket is full. At the exit she queues up at one of several cash desks and pays for all the goods she has bought.

2.翻译下面的句子,注意同形异类词的译词选择。

(1) The shops are always crowded on Saturdays.

There are large crowds of people in the streets on Saturdays.

(2) My neighbour was talked into buying a TV set last week.

He gave an interesting talk to the students about his travel in China.

(3) Did you say you were thirty-nine? But you don't look it at all.

There were angry looks from the passersby when he was found responsible for the road accident.

(4) The company publishes more than two hundred books every year.

Seats for the cinema can be booked from 8:30 am to 5 pm.

(5) Only 50 *yuan* for a pair of shoes? What a good buy!

I am going to buy myself a new car for my birthday.

3. 翻译下面的句子,注意译文中从句的位置。

(1) My husband looks after the kids while I do the weekend shopping here.

(2) If the answer is wrong, give what you think is correct.

(3) Return the novel to the library if you have finished with it.

(4) It was raining heavily when they came back.

(5) You'll get yourself talked about if you behave badly.

(6) I'd like to ask you a few questions if you can spare me thirty minutes for an interview.

Lesson 6
Right or Left

Which of your two hands do you use most? Very few of us can use both of our hands equally well. Most of us are right-handed. Only about five people out of a hundred are left-handed.[①] Newborn babies can grasp objects with either of their hands, but in about two years they usually prefer to use their right hands. Scientists don't know why this happens. They used to think that we inherited this tendency from our animal ancestors[②], but this may not be true. Monkeys are our closest relatives in the animal world. Scientists have found that monkeys prefer to use one of their hands more than the other—but it can be either hand. There are as many right-handed monkeys as there are left-handed ones.[③] Next time you visit the zoo, watch the monkeys carefully. You will see that some of them will prefer to swing from their right hands and others will use their left hands. But most human beings use their right hands better and this makes life difficult for those who prefer to use their left hands.[④] We live in a right-handed world.

● 注　释 ●

① Only about five people out of a hundred are left-handed.
大约只有 5% 的人是左撇子。

② we inherited this tendency from our animal ancestors.
这一习惯是我们从动物祖先那儿继承下来的。

③ There are as many right-handed monkeys as there are left-handed ones.
习惯使用右前肢的猴子数目与使用左前肢的一样多。

④ this makes life difficult for those who prefer to use their left hands.
这给喜欢用左手的人的生活带来诸多不便。

※ 译词分析 ※

"from"的翻译
英语介词"from"的汉语译词很多。现在将 1～6 课课文和练习中带"from"的句子译法归纳如下：

1. 把"from"译为"从"，如：

◇ She moves from counter to counter, from shelf to shelf, selecting her groceries, her meat, her vegetables, even sometimes her crockery or clothes, until her basket is full.

她从一个柜台到另一个柜台，从一个货架到另一个货架选购商品，肉啦、青菜啦，有时还买瓦罐啦、衣服啦，直到篮子塞满为止。

◇ They used to think that we inherited this tendency from our ancestors.

他们过去认为这一习性是我们从动物祖先那儿继承下来的。

2. 把"from"译为"跟"，如：

◇ It's quite different from what I thought.

这跟我原来想像的完全不同。

3. "from"与名词或动词组合的词组，不一定都有通用的固定译法，应从其语义、搭配关系和上下文中去考虑具体的译词选择。例如：

◇ This is Riaz from Pakistan.

这位是来自巴基斯坦的里亚兹。

◇ The thunderstorm saves the flowers from midsummer scorching.

雷阵雨使鲜花免受仲夏烈日的蒸晒。

◇ swing from their right hands

用右前肢荡秋千

※ 译法分析 ※

同形同类词的翻译

这里要谈的是一词多义和一词多译的问题。有的同形同类英语词语有多个译词，例如"supermarket"，译为"超级市场"（超市）或"自选市场"都可以。有的同形同类英语词语，由于所在句子的语体不同、搭配用法或者修辞要求有差别，翻译成汉语时译词的选择也会有所不同。照抄辞典不符合上述原则，千万慎重。例如：

1. 语体差别

◇ if — 假若，如果，要是

◇ shopping — 买东西，购物

2. 搭配差别

◇ left-handed people — 左撇子

◇ right-handed monkeys — 习惯使用右前肢的猴子

◇ two hands — 双手

◇ two years — 两年

◇ you two — 你们二位

3. 地域差别

◇ taxi — 出租汽车,的士(多用于南方沿海城市),计程车(多用于台湾)

4. 语义差别(以"get"为例)

◇ Now what can I get you?
给您来点什么?

◇ You'll get used to everything here in a year or two.
过一两年你对这里的一切都会习惯的。

◇ I haven't got over it yet.
我还没有缓过劲儿来。

◇ How did you get on in the match?
那场比赛打得怎么样?

 练 习

1. 翻译短文:

Which is better — to drive on the left or the right? A team of scientists say that cars driving on the right-hand side of the road probably help make tornadoes. They say that cars and trucks going very fast past each other make the air turn anticlockwise. The air in tornadoes turns anticlockwise in the northern hemisphere. So cars in the U.S.A. must drive on the left. There are about 2.5 million cars and lorries moving on the roads at any moment. The air that they move is probably enough to change the movement of the atmosphere.

2. 翻译下面的句子,注意"get"的译法。

(1) You can get almost anywhere in this city by bus or underground railway.

(2) Have you got a ticket for tonight's show?

(3) I'll come and see you if I get time.

(4) The boy is getting along well in school.

(5) How many stations can you get on your radio set?

(6) "Go and get your breakfast," said the mother.

(7) I can't get anyone to do the work properly.

(8) What beautiful teeth he's got!

3. 完成下面句子的翻译,注意"from"的译法。

(1) I have just received a letter from my brother.

我刚刚收到_____。

(2) He never borrows any money from his friends.

他从不_____借钱。

(3) Apart from a few words, I do not know any French.

_____我一点法语都不懂。

(4) He refused a strange request from a businessman.

他拒绝了_____。

(5) They were the first group of the passengers who directly flew from London.

他们是第一批_____的旅客。

(6) The supermarket is only five miles away from our college.

超市_____只有五英里。

4. 选词填空:

(1) Please tell us the names of the objects in this room.

请告诉我们房间里的这些_____都叫什么。

    A.物体   B.对象   C.目标   D.东西

(2) What would you prefer: rice or dumplings?

你_____吃什么:米饭还是饺子?

    A.喜欢   B.比较喜欢   C.更喜欢   D.最喜欢

(3) Could I use your Chinese-English Dictionary?

我可以_____一下你的《汉英词典》吗?

    A.用   B.应用   C.运用   D.利用

(4) Be more careful with your homework.

你做家庭作业要更_____些。

    A.当心   B.精心   C.认真   D.小心

(5) The twin sisters are equally clever.

这对孪生姐妹_____聪明。

    A.相同   B.一样   C.平等   D.相等

Lesson 7
Translation as a Subject

下面是中外师生之间关于翻译问题的一次谈话,学习翻译课的学生不妨读一读,也许会有所帮助。

问:什么是翻译?

答:把一种语言的一个词或词组的含义、一个句子或一段话的意思、一篇文章或一本书的内容,用另一种语言的口头或书面形式或同一种语言的另一种形式表达出来,就叫做"翻译"。

问:为什么要学习翻译课?

答:要学好一门外语必须掌握"听"、"说"、"读"、"写"、"译"五种技能。根据个人的条件、专业和兴趣,每个学生在这五个方面都可以有所侧重,但是最好不要偏废,都应该打下良好基础,否则他的外语知识和技能就可能存在缺陷。外语学习是一种跨语言的活动,学生往往自觉或不自觉地在两种语言比较和翻译中学习提高,初级阶段尤其是这样。选修英汉翻译课可以使自己的汉语知识更加丰富,运用汉语的能力得到进一步提高。

问:努力学习各门汉语课程,是不是就自然而然会翻译了?

答:不一定。用外语交流思想与两种语言之间的互译是两个不同的概念。从某种意义上说,"翻译"是一门学问,一种技巧,从专业高度上说也是一种专门艺术,不经过学习训练是无法获得的。会游泳的人不一定都是潜水员。有些外国人在中国生活了几十年,中国人说话他们大体上都明白,但是他们也许看不懂报纸,更不会翻译,因为他们没有系统地学习过汉语。这说明学什么才能懂什么。

问:能不能举例说明学习翻译课的必要性?

答:几十年前一位中国学者把"the Milky Way"翻译成"牛奶路",鲁迅批评说哪有什么"牛奶路",应该译为"银河"或者"天河"。在汉语的词汇中的确没有"牛奶路",这样翻译一般人都看不懂,因此鲁迅的批评是有道理的。但是半个世纪后有些翻译家说要是当时那位学者把它翻译成"天上的牛奶路",也许人们就能理解了,因为别的语言使用而我们不使用的表达形式就是这样通过翻译作品介绍过来的,不必大惊小怪。可见,翻译理论和方法不是固定不变的,它总是随着语言的发展、人们对翻译性质的认识和对技巧研究的深入而发展。光懂得句子中每一个词的意思不一定就能胜任翻译工作,这里有理论、方法、技巧和经验的问题。

问：将来不想从事翻译工作也要学习翻译课吗？

答：你有选择的自由，不过翻译课既然是一门课自然有它的特点。通过两种语言的比较和翻译，可以从另一个角度加深对汉语的语音、词汇、语法和文化的理解，扩大汉语知识面，提高汉语口头和书面表达的熟练程度。汉外对比可以帮助我们总结出一些规律性的东西。比如汉语的定语和状语都应该放在中心语之前，而英语却可以放在中心语之前或者之后，这样的对比在汉语语法课中可以不专门讲解，但是在汉英对译中却必须涉及。翻译课中学习的内容有助于大家学好其他课程，而其他课程却无法替代翻译课。

问：翻译课是不是一门枯燥的理论课？

答：不是。翻译课主要是一门实践课，内容具体，涉及到两种语言的表达和社会生活的方方面面，一点也不枯燥。老师有时要讲一些理论，但理论是用于总结规律，都离不开例子。有时还要用英语和汉语对等的表达方式进行比较，也都跟实际应用有关。

问：语音、词汇和语法，哪一方面的知识对学好翻译课更重要？

答：翻译课可以分为口译课和笔译课，本阶段开设的翻译课主要涉及到对原文的理解和译文表达中的词汇、语法、修辞和文化背景问题，其中词汇和语法尤为重要。但是全面并熟练掌握两种语言的各种知识是学好翻译课所必须的。

问：对比研究对于学习翻译课有多大帮助？

答：对比研究的范围可以包括语音对比、词法对比、句法对比和文化对比。在方法上对比研究也可以分为理论对比和应用对比，宏观对比和微观对比，历时对比和共时对比。《英汉翻译教程》（第一册）涉及的主要是词法、句法和文化的基础应用对比。对比教学可以帮助学生了解汉英同类结构或者表达方式的异同点，从而能更准确地把握汉语，提高熟练程度。仅仅做翻译练习是不够的，碰到相同的语言现象不能举一反三。

问：文化差异会影响译者对原文的理解和译文的准确性吗？

答：回答是肯定的。所谓"文化"，在翻译中主要涉及背景知识和思维表达方式。不懂中国的历史、地理、政治、哲学、宗教和风俗习惯，就谈不上精通汉语。"盘古开天地"、"事后诸葛亮"、"借东风"、"行行出状元"等许多词语，外国留学生仅仅从字面意思是无法理解其丰富含义的。中国人为什么说"东南西北"、"男女老少"，而不说"北西南东"、"少女老男"？这里有约定俗成的问题，也有文化背景和思维方式的问题。缺乏这方面的知识，准确理解或翻译汉语就会有困难。

问：什么样的译文是好译文？

答：中国翻译家严复在《天演论·译例言》中说："译事三难：信达雅。"用现在的话来说，好的翻译应该体现在三个方面：忠实原文的意思，准确表达，语法通顺,易读易懂,译文的风格和用词与原作的体裁和思想基本一致。由于个人的理解能力不同,语言表达技巧的差异,翻译内容、方式(口译或笔译)、场合等因素的区别,实际翻译时不可能只有一个模式。同样一篇文章,不同的人有不同的译文,甚至同一个人在不同时间的译文也不尽相同。不同的人对翻译标准可能有不同的见解,但是对于翻译的原则、方法和效果多数人的看法是一致的。

◎ 思 考 题 ◎

1. 学习翻译课的目的和意义是什么?
2. 翻译课对学好汉语有什么帮助?
3. 翻译课与汉语其他课程是怎样相辅相成的?
4. 学习翻译课要克服哪些困难?
5. 怎样才能学好翻译课?

Lesson 8
The Guitar

The people of the world speak different languages, but everyone understands one special language — music. In Africa, Asia, Australia, America or Europe, people sing or play musical instruments. There are many kinds of musical instruments, but one is famous all over the world — the guitar. Everyone can understand the music of the guitar, and nearly everyone likes its sound. Guitar music is a world language, and the guitar is the most popular instrument in the world.

The guitar has a long history. In ancient Egypt people played a simple stringed instrument like the guitar. The Greeks and the Romans made music by plucking strings with their fingers.① The first guitar appeared during the fifteenth century in Spain. At first it was an instrument for poor people and traveling musicians②, but soon rich people all over Europe were learning to play the guitar.

In the modern world there are four kinds of guitar: the classical, the flamenco, the steel-stringed and the electric guitar. Today the guitar is played in cafes, at parties, in concert halls and at pop festivals. At any hour of the day or night someone somewhere is playing the guitar.③

● 注　　释 ●

① The Greeks and the Romans made music by plucking strings with their fingers.
希腊人和罗马人用手指拨动琴弦弹奏乐曲。
② traveling musicians
江湖艺人;巡游乐师
③ At any hour of the day or night someone somewhere is playing the guitar.
无论是白天还是晚上的任何时候总有一些地方总有一些人在弹奏吉他。

※ 译词分析 ※

"make"的翻译
英语动词"make"的搭配能力非常强,是一个多义项的动词,翻译时要从辞典中找出一个现成的译词往往很困难,需要仔细辨别其含义,慎重选词。比较一下第 1 课至第 8 课课文和练习中带"make"的一些句子的翻译就可以了解到这一情况:

◇ The Greeks and the Romans made music by plucking strings with their fingers.
希腊人和罗马人用手指拨动琴弦弹奏乐曲。

◇ We don't want to make any mistake, do we?
我们不想犯什么错误,对吧?

◇ Oily hair makes a student like me look funny.
像我这样的学生头发油光锃亮的看起来有点滑稽可笑。

◇ This makes life difficult for those who prefer to use their left hands.
这给喜欢用左手的人的生活带来诸多不便。

◇ Cars driving on the right-hand side of the road probably help make tornadoes.
在马路右边开车可能会促使旋风的形成。

※ 译法分析 ※

英语动词过去分词的翻译

英语动词的过去分词用来表示性质和状态时,多半放在所修饰的名词之前,跟汉语的定语位置完全相同。

当过去分词用来表示动作行为的完成或者被动时,也可以放在被修饰的名词之后。汉译时,一般都应把它译为作定语的动词,放在所修饰名词之前。

◇ I came to enjoy wheeling my trolley round, inspecting the shelves *stocked* high with goods.
我渐渐地喜欢推着小车四下里转,巡视着高高码着货物的架子。

把表示完成和被动的英语及物动词的过去分词译成汉语时,译词应该按照汉语习惯进行搭配。例如:

◇ newborn babies   新生儿
◇ fallen leaves   落叶
◇ mixed doubles   混合双打
◇ spoken French   法语口语
◇ stringed instrument   弦乐器
◇ steel-stringed guitar   钢丝吉他
◇ a right-handed world   使用右手者的世界

══════ 练　　习 ══════

1. 翻译短文:

Recently the keeper of our local inn bought a very curious musical instrument

25

from one of his customers. It can best be described as a large music-box. It is over six feet tall and there is a small window at the top through which can be seen a number of wheels with small metal teeth. As soon as the instrument is wound up by means of a handle at the side, the wheels go round and play three charming little tunes. As the bell-like tunes are very faint, you have to listen carefully to hear them. The old-fashioned music-box has caused a lot of excitement in our village and has already attracted a large number of visitors.

2. 翻译下列词组,注意过去分词的译法。

    （1）an unknown number   （2）an unemployed woman
    （3）a determined effort   （4）detailed description
    （5）the safely preserved treasure   （6）the candied fruit
    （7）some cancelled tickets   （8）the chosen books
    （9）a closed cabin   （10）the cultivated land
   （11）the exhausted tea   （12）a finished product
   （13）a hidden danger   （14）a shaped coat

3. 翻译下列句子,注意过去分词的译法。

    （1）Pupils always have to be well-behaved at schools.
    （2）When Anna began to work as an assistant in a record shop, Judy, an experienced girl, was there to guide her.
    （3）The castle was built for an American named William Randolph Hearst.
    （4）Tom, aged 18, is now in the sitting-room waiting for his mother.
    （5）On the wall is a photo taken in Paris last year.
    （6）If the population of the earth goes on increasing, there will eventually not be enough resources left to sustain life on the planet.

4. 翻译下列带动词"make"的句子:

    （1）Many hands make light work.
    （2）You can make friends with the Chinese speakers in the club.
    （3）Mr. Wang made little of his saving the drowning child.
    （4）His explanation made no sense.
    （5）They made up their minds to buy a car.
    （6）Don't make fun of the girl behind her back.

Lesson 9
Tea Drinking

Tea is drunk widely all over the world. It originated in China about 2700 B.C.

The manner in which people prepare and drink their tea differs in different parts of the world. Some people drink tea plain. Others like to add milk and sugar or lemon juice. A few people like to add rum, Scotch, or cognac to their tea.

In Tibet a cup of tea is served with a lump of yak butter floating on its surface.[1] The Tibetans are so fond of this that they drink at least 10 or 20 cups every day.

The Russians usually take lump sugar with their tea. In olden days the peasants rarely placed the sugar in their tea, but held it between their teeth as they drank.[2]

The Japanese have special ritual in serving tea. It is called *chanoyu*[3]. The tea is meticulously prepared and is accompanied by a variety of delicate seasonal dishes.[4] The conversation, the setting, and even the colours and shapes of teapots are carefully calculated to achieve the most harmonious and satisfying effect.[5]

● 注　　释 ●

[1] In Tibet a cup of tea is served with a lump of yak butter floating on its surface.
在西藏,一杯茶端上来时表面上总是浮着一块酥油。

[2] but held it between their teeth as they drank.
而是咬着糖块喝茶。

[3] *chanoyu*
茶道

[4] is accompanied by a variety of delicate seasonal dishes.
还配上各种应时美味小吃。

[5] to achieve the most harmonious and satisfying effect.
以达到最和谐、最满意的效果。

※ 译法分析 ※

"it"和"its"的翻译

英语单数第三人称代词"it"和形容词性单数第三人称物主代词"its",与汉语的人称代词"它"和表领属关系的"它的",有相同之处,也有不同之处。翻译时有四种情况:1.译出来;2.不译出来;3.可译可不译;4.把它还原为所指代的事物。现在分别举例说明如下:

1. 把"it"和"its"译出来

◇ At first it was an instrument for poor people and traveling musicians, but soon rich people all over Europe were learning to play the guitar.

开始时它是一种穷人和巡游乐师玩的乐器,但是很快地全欧洲的富人也学起了吉他。

2. "it"省译

用来表示时间、距离、自然现象或指人时,以及作形式主语、表示强调的主语、形式宾语或语助词时,通常可以不译出来。例如:

◇ Was it very cold last winter?

去年冬天冷吗?

◇ Don't mention it.

不谢。

◇ Do you still find it a great trouble to get up in the morning?

你现在早晨起床还觉得费劲吗?

◇ The Japanese have special ritual in serving tea. It is called *chanoyu*.

日本人献茶都有特定的仪式,(这)叫茶道。

3. 还原所指代的事物

"它"可以用来表示单数也可以用来表示复数,因此在翻译中有时要把"it"或"its"还原为所指代的事物,以免意思含混不清。一般说来,汉语中"它"的使用频率不如英语中高,这也是其中一个原因。请比较:

◇ In olden days the peasants rarely placed the sugar lump in their tea, but held it between their teeth as they drank.

早先农民很少在茶里放糖块,而是咬着糖块喝茶。

◇ My spoken French was terrible and I was afraid to use it in shops.

我法语讲得很糟,害怕到商店买东西时讲法语。

以上翻译方法也基本适用于表示事物的代词"they"及与其对应的物主代词"their"。

1. 翻译短文：

Coffee houses became popular in America when settlers from Europe brought the idea with them. Coffee soon became the leading American drink. Today people in the United States drink coffee at breakfast, at lunch, at dinner, and between meals. They drink hot coffee and coffee with ice in it. They drink at work and at home. They eat coffee ice cream and coffee candy.

Coffee is drunk by people around the world. Some people like coffee that is black and very strong. Other people like coffee with cream or sugar in it. In all the ways coffee is served, it has become an international drink.

2. 翻译下面的句子，注意"it"的译法。

(1) Some students find it difficult to understand English slang.

(2) Don't take it amiss if I say that you are allowing your ambition to run riot.

(3) I leave it to you to make up your own mind.

(4) It is embarrassing not being able to understand what people say to you.

(5) The path was so slippery that we couldn't walk along it.

(6) We won't go out unless it stops raining.

(7) Well may you say that it is too late to do anything about it now.

(8) Legend tells us that a Chinese Empress, while taking her tea, dipped the cocoon of a silk-worm into it and learned how to unwind the fine thread of silk of which it was composed.

3. 完成下面句子的翻译：

(1) One day she visited a travel bureau to ask about the qualifications for a tourist guide.

有一天她去一家旅行社打听_____。

(2) Like many other city people, they have found it hard to live without machines.

就像许多城市居民一样，他们也觉得_____。

(3) Besides gathering and storing information, the computer can also solve complicated problems that once took months for people to do.

除了收集和储存信息外，计算机还能_____。

(4) Drastic measures must be taken if we want to reduce traffic accidents, traffic congestion and air pollution.

如果我们想要＿＿＿＿＿＿＿＿＿＿＿＿＿＿＿＿＿＿＿＿就必须采取严厉措施。

(5) Strong winds bent the grass near the beach, and the smell of salt air came in from the sea.

大风＿＿＿＿＿＿＿＿＿＿海滩边上的青草，从海上＿＿＿＿＿＿＿＿＿＿＿＿。

(6) Many mountaineers wanted to climb the top of Jolmo Lungma, and many of them lost their lives there.

许多登山运动员曾经想攀登珠穆朗玛峰＿＿＿＿＿＿＿＿＿＿＿＿。

Lesson 10
The Longest River

Did you know that the River Nile[①] is not the longest river in the world? For many years people have thought it was. It appears in all the old reference books as being longer than the Amazon.[②] But in 1953 the true source of the Amazon was found to be a stream called Huaraco in Peru. In 1969 some scientists re-measured the length of the river and found it to be 6,712 km long.

The most authoritative survey of the Nile was made by a Belgian in 1916. He reckoned that its length was 6,632 km. Since then Lake Nasser has been filled up. The Nile used to wind its way through this area.[③] The Nile is therefore shorter now. Consequently it is more than 80 km shorter than the Amazon.

But the matter is not quite as simple as that.[④] It depends on which channel of the Amazon delta you choose. If you choose the shortest one, which is not often used, the length of the Amazon is only 6,411 km. So perhaps the Nile is still the longest river in the world.

● 注　　释 ●

① the（River）Nile　　尼罗河　　　　the Amazon　　亚马孙河
　 Huaraco　　　　　 华拉科小河　Peru　　　　　秘鲁
　 Belgian　　　　　 比利时人　　Lake Nasser　 纳赛尔湖

② It appears in all the old reference books as being longer than the Amazon.
　 在所有老参考书的记载中它是一条比亚马孙河长的河。

③ The Nile used to wind its way through this area.
　 尼罗河曾经蜿蜒流过这个地区。

④ But the matter is not quite as simple as that.
　 但是事情并不那么简单。

※ 译法分析 ※

词的音译和音意合译

当译入语中没有与原语相同或近似意义的对应词时,就可以采用发音近似的音节(在汉语中用汉字)来拼读原文中的那些词。这种翻译方法就是"音译"。音译词多半是人名或地名等专有名词,但也可能是普通名词,甚至其他词类或词组。

音译词可以分为下列两大类:

一、音译词,例如:

Washington	华盛顿	Peter	彼得
salad	色拉	coffee	咖啡
kowtow	叩头	sampan	舢板

二、音意合译词,例如:

1. 将原词部分音译部分意译:

| the River Nile | 尼罗河 | Lake Nasser 纳赛尔湖 |
| New Delhi | 新德里 | |

2. 将原词音译后加上意译成分:

the Amazon	亚马孙河	Scotch	苏格兰威士忌
rum	朗姆酒	cognac	科涅克酒
jazz	爵士乐	jeep	吉普车

音译词语时有几点值得注意:

A. 有些词语在原文中本来就是音译词,汉译时可以音译也可以意译,需酌情而定,例如"*chanoyu*",汉译为"茶道"。

B. 许多音译词已有约定俗成的译法。如"西藏"通常英译为"Tibet","广州"过去英译为"Canton",现在按照汉语拼音统一译为"Guangzhou"。

C. 把英语词语音译成汉语时,应尽可能选择常用汉字,字数不宜过多,字面意思不使人产生错误联想。

═══════ 练　　习 ═══════

1. 翻译短文:

No one before had conquered the whole of the powerful, mysterious Amazon. A team of explorers were going to mount boats and go down one of the most dangerous rivers in the world. The expedition would begin in August 1985 with a climb to the source of the Amazon, a snowfield high in the Andes. Once in the jungle they would switch to sea kayaks for 3700 miles through the Amazon basin to the Atlantic. A general practitioner in London gave the team a special medical kit to prevent or nurse the members through malaria, rabies and other horrors. It would be a great adventure to pit them against their own limits. If they succeed they would be the first ever to trace the earth's largest river from its source to the sea.

2. 翻译下面的句子,注意数字的译法。

(1) Mr. Jackson, 147 Draton Green, Eastfield, Brighton YN4 7BC

Arriving 6 A.M. Monday. Saran.

(2) The population of Quebec in the 1976 census was 177,082. Almost 92% of the people are of French origin, and 99% are French-speaking.

(3) Each academic year is divided into three terms. Staff members take a month off at Christmas and Easter and eight weeks in the summer.

(4) Of the $1,311 family food bill in 1972, middlemen received $790, which was thirty-three per cent more than they had received in 1959.

(5) Furnished sublet, large 3 bed-room apt., comfortable for three. 10 min. walk to the college. Apr. 1 – Aug. 31. $459.99/month each & electricity. Tel. 4732256.

3. 用音译或音意合译方法翻译下列词和词组:

(1) Los Angeles (2) Thames Television
(3) Mrs. Morales (4) Dr. Cheyney
(5) Fiji Times (6) Canada
(7) the City of London (8) butter
(9) the Nobel Prizes

Lesson 11
Back to the Bike

Private cars or public transport — it's the same thing. Traveling to work gets more difficult and more expensive every year. Ordinary people can do nothing about the world price of petrol, or a national rise in fares.[①] They have to get to work, so they have to pay. People are looking for cheaper kinds of transport, and they have found one from the past. They are going back to the bike[②].

Children often go to school by bike and students cycle to class. But now businessmen are going to the office by bike. "The bicycle," said Mr. Brown[③], "is a businessman's dream. It's easy to make and it's cheap. You can buy thirty bikes for the price of one small car. A bike doesn't use expensive fuel, like petrol, but runs on manpower. You don't have large bills for repairs — a child of ten can learn to look after a bicycle.[④] And most bikes will last a lifetime."

"Cycling is good for you," added Mr. Williams[⑤]. "Drivers sit in traffic jams and get angry. That's bad for the heart. Then they can't find a place to park and get angrier. And many of them get fat too. If you cycle to work you save petrol, save money and save your health. And you often save time too."

Cycling is clean, quiet, cheap and healthy. And it can also be fun. You can cycle to work all week and go for a cycle ride in the countryside at the weekend. You can also go on a cycling holiday.

● 注　释 ●

① Ordinary people can do nothing about the world price of petrol, or a national rise in fares.
老百姓对于世界性的汽油价格和全国性的车票提价都无能为力。

② going back to the bike
再次骑起自行车

③ Mr. Brown
布朗先生

④ a child of ten can learn to look after a bicycle.
一个 10 岁的孩子都能学会保养自行车。

⑤ Mr. Williams
    威廉斯先生

※ 译词分析 ※

"or"的翻译

现在把所学过课文中"or"的几种汉语译法小结如下:

1. 在叙述句中表示选择,译为"或者"或"或"。例如:

◇ A few people like to add rum, Scotch, *or* cognac to their tea.
    一些人喜欢在茶里加朗姆酒、苏格兰威士忌或者法国白兰地。

◇ The roads were covered with slippery ice *or* deep snow.
    路上覆盖着滑滑的冰或厚厚的雪。

2. 在疑问句中表示选择,译为"还是"。例如:

◇ What's the best season in Beijing: spring *or* autumn?
    北京最好的季节是春天还是秋天?

3. 用来覆盖两种以上相似或者相反情况时,可以译为"无论……或者"或"不管……还是"。例如:

◇ Private cars or public transport — it's the same thing.
    不管是私人汽车还是公共运输公司,情况都一样。

◇ Ordinary people can do nothing about the world price of petrol, or a national rise in fares.
    老百姓对于世界性的汽油价格和全国性的车票提价都无能为力。

4. "or"用于连接两个相邻的数字,意思相近或相反的名词时,可以将那些数字或名词直接译出,"or"则不必择词另译。例如:

◇ 10 or 20 cups   10～20 杯
◇ a year or two   一两年

※ 译法分析 ※

英语名词复数的翻译

1. 带数量修饰语的英语名词复数,一般都应该按汉语名词复数的表达方式(如:表示 2 以上的数词＋量词＋名词,或者表示频度的形容词和副词＋名词)准确译出。例如:

◇ three fine eighteenth-century houses   三座漂亮的 18 世纪老楼
◇ 33℃   33 摄氏度
◇ for many years   多年来

◇ a few people 　　　　　　　　　一些人
◇ some of my records 　　　　　　我的几张唱片
◇ all the ponds, lakes and rivers 　所有的池塘、湖泊和河流
◇ different parts of the world 　　世界各地

　　也有一些英语复数名词,虽然不带数量修饰语,但是根据上下文的语义逻辑和汉语语法要求,必须明确地把它的复数含义翻译出来。

　　下面是已学课文中的几个例子:

◇ cheap kinds of transport
　　各种经济实惠的交通工具

◇ Children often go to school by bike and students cycle to class.
　　孩子们经常骑自行车上学,学生们也骑自行车去上课。

◇ I came to enjoy wheeling my trolley round, inspecting the shelves stocked high with goods.
　　我渐渐地喜欢推着小车四下里转,看看那些高高地码着货物的架子。

　　2. 有些英语名词,虽然其语法形式是复数的,但是不带数量修饰语或只带无明确单复数界限的修饰语,汉译时可以用无单复数标志的名词把它翻译出来。例如:

◇ Bitter north winds stripped all trees of their leaves.
　　寒冷的北风刮落了所有树上的叶子。

◇ Newborn babies can grasp objects with either of their hands.
　　刚出生不久的婴儿能用任何一只手抓东西。

━━━━━━ 练　　习 ━━━━━━

1. 翻译短文:

　　The bicycle is one of the most useful inventions. Ninety years ago, men rode on a heavy and dangerous kind of bicycle with a rather larger wheel in front and a small one at the back. The front wheel was as high as six feet and the one at the back of it was only a few inches in diameter. When the present bicycle with two wheels of the same size was invented, it was called a "safety", because people were so much safer sitting on a seat four feet from the ground than on six or seven feet above the road. Even then riding on a bicycle was not so comfortable as the tyres were made of solid rubber. Later someone discovered the use of air-filled tyres and this helped to make the bicycle what it was today.

2. 选择一个适当词语翻译下面的句子：

　　　大约　　或者　　还是　　要不

（1）Shall we help him or leave him alone?

（2）Some children pedal their tricycles, but most of them prefer to push or drag them.

（3）If you bought a car or stove those days, it was considered a lifelong investment.

（4）There will be twenty or so people at the party.

（5）Look sharp, or you'll be late for work.

3. 用恰当的数量修饰语翻译下面的短语：

（1）twenty-five students in the room　　　（2）many tall trees in the jungle

（2）more than two months　　　（4）those houses built of stone

（5）some high mountains　　　（6）several new books

（7）a big collection of books　　　（8）untold wealth

（9）countless stars in the sky　　　（10）tickets for everyone

（11）no end of trouble　　　（12）six hours on end

Lesson 12
The Pleasure of Picnics

Some people have always had to eat away from home[①]— farm workers in the fields, hunters in the forests, and travelers on the road. Others choose to eat in the open air. They take their lunch or tea out into the countryside and have a picnic.

The strange word "picnic" which was once spelled "Pick Nick" used to mean a dinner party with different dishes brought by each participant. "A picnic supper," says *The Times*[②] of March 18th, 1802, "consists of many different dishes. Before the night each guest receives a menu with a number against one dish. Then he has to provide the dish marked with his number."

These picnic suppers were usually held indoors in well decorated dining rooms, but sometimes tables were laid outside in the gardens of stately homes. Soon "picnic" came to mean any outdoor party with food.[③] In the summer months both rich and poor people went out into the woods and fields for May Day and Midsummer picnics. When workers moved from the country to new jobs in the towns, they returned at weekends for picnics — food tastes better in the fresh air. And they needed a rest from the noise and dirt of the cities.[④]

Today picnics are as popular as ever, ordinary family picnics or splendid outdoor parties are held when the weather is good.

● 注　　释 ●

① Some people have always had to eat away from home.
有些人总是不能在家吃饭。

② *The Times*
《泰晤士报》

③ Soon "picnic" came to mean any outdoor party with food.
不久"picnic"的意思就成了"室外的聚餐"。

④ And they needed a rest from the noise and dirt of the cities.
而且他们也需要在远离都市喧嚣和污浊的环境中休息一下。

※ 译词分析 ※

"take"的翻译

前面所学课文中"take"有以下几种译法：

◇ Let me take your coat.

把衣服给我吧。

◇ It won't take you long to settle down here.

用不了多长时间你就会在这儿安定下来。

◇ We'll take a taxi.

我们要坐出租汽车。

◇ Could you please take a little more off the sides?

请把边上的头发理掉一些,行吗?

◇ The Russians usually take lump sugar with their tea.

俄国人一般都在茶里加方糖。

◇ You could be taken to a police station if your driving has been affected by alcohol.

如果你喝酒影响了开车,就可能被带到警察局去。

◇ They take their lunch or tea out into the countryside and have a picnic.

他们把午饭或茶点带到乡下去野餐。

 练 习

1. 翻译短文：

"Let's go for a picnic," said Mrs. Smith.

"Yes, let's go to the woods and have our picnic there," said Mr. Smith.

With the help of their two children, Mary and John, they soon got everything ready. They drove along small roads until they came to the woods. Mary put the blanket on the ground, John took the food out of the car, Father made a fire, and Mother made tea.

"Isn't it beautiful here?" said Mother. "It's quiet and green."

John had a kite, and soon he was across the grass with it.

"Be careful!" shouted Mother, but it was late. John fell over the basket of food, and everything fell out.

2. 从所给词语中选择一个适当的翻译下列句子：

(1) The <u>subjects</u> that he studied in school included Chinese, mathematics, physics, chemistry, geography, English and music. （题目，课程，问题，主语）

(2) He was so successful that he was able to <u>open</u> his own school when he was only twenty-five. （打开，睁开，开办，开设）

(3) They <u>built</u> a machine that people could use to talk to one another over long distance. （制造，建筑，建立，建设）

(4) A large brown hen was <u>scratching</u> in the dirt in the barnyard with her four chicks. （扒，抓，擦，刮）

(5) Scientists have found that almost every species of animal has a communication <u>system</u>. （制度，系统，体系，体制）

(6) A car that is <u>taken care of</u> will work well for years. （照顾，保养，照料，处理）

(7) Proteins, vitamins, minerals, carbohydrates, <u>fats</u> and water are the six main groups of nutrients that a human body needs. （肥肉，油脂，脂肪，油料）

3. 翻译下列句子，注意"take"在句子中的确切含义。

(1) Let us take our spades and dig deeply to turn over the soil.

(2) He offered to take care of the children while their parents are away from home.

(3) We will take a chance on the weather and have the party outdoors.

(4) Annie took advantage of lunch hour to finish her homework.

(5) Take it easy. The roads are icy.

(6) A helicopter is able to take off and land straight up or down.

(7) The secretary takes many letters to the post every day.

Lesson 13
Long Life

Did you know that there have been only 14 people that have lived for more than 110 years? There have been thousands of claims to longer life than 110 years, but there is reliable proof for only 14.[①]

What is the oldest age to which any human being has ever lived? If we believe the Bible, Methuselah[②] died at the age of 969 years. If we believe Chinese legend, Li Chungyun was born in 1680 and died in 1933. If we believe Russian legend, Sherali was born in 1805 and was still alive in 1973. But scientists do not believe any of these claims.

It is very difficult to be sure of the age of very old people. The official registration of birth has not been compulsory in many countries. In England it was not made completely compulsory till 1874. In the U.S.A. it was not compulsory till 1920. In many of the old Chinese clanbooks the birth of each member was recorded[③], but they were not for official use, and sometimes failed to be correct.

Why do some people live to a healthy old age?[④] What is the secret of their long lives? Three things seem to be very important: fresh air, fresh food and a simple way of life.

● 注　　释 ●

① but there is reliable proof for only 14.
   但是只有 14 个人的情况得到了证实。
② Methuselah　　　　麦修塞拉
   Li Chungyun　　　　李钟云
   Sherali　　　　舍拉利
③ In many of the old Chinese clanbooks the birth of each member was recorded.
   在中国过去许多族谱中记载着每一个成员的出生时间。
④ Why do some people live to a healthy old age?
   为什么有些人能健康长寿？

※ 译词分析 ※

"people"的翻译

英语"people"有多个对等汉语译词,但是其中三个,即"人"、"人们"和"人民",外国留学生往往混淆。现在对这些用法分别说明如下:

1. 把"people"译为"人"。汉语"人"用于泛指人类社会成员,可以是单数概念,也可以是复数概念。例如:

◇ rich people   富人
◇ some people   某些人
◇ ordinary people   普通人
◇ a few people   一些人
◇ very old people   年纪很大的人
◇ five people   五个人

2. 把"people"译为"人们"。汉语"人们"是复数概念的名词,泛指"许多人"。例如:

◇ For many years people have thought that the River Nile was the longest river in the world.

多年来人们一直认为尼罗河是世界上最长的河。

◇ People are looking for cheaper kinds of transport.

人们在寻找各种经济实惠的交通工具。

3. 把"people"译为"人民"。汉语"人民"包含复数概念,泛指社会、国家或民族中的基本成员。例如:

◇ Chinese people   中国人民
◇ the People's Republic of China 中华人民共和国
◇ working people   劳动人民

※ 译法分析 ※

英语时量词语的翻译

英语表示生命、动作或状态延续时间的长度,可以用定语、表语或状语及其相应的从句。译成汉语时,一般可以用表示时量的定语、状语或者补语。例如:

◇ I've been learning Chinese at this university since 1998.

从 1998 年到现在我一直在这所大学学习汉语。

◇ Other provinces are warm all the year round and have no real winter.

其他省份一年四季都很暖和,没有真正的冬天。

◇ Did you know that the River Nile is not the longest river in the world? For many years people have thought it was.

你是否知道尼罗河并不是世界上最长的河？多年来人们曾经以为它是。

这类汉语译句中谓语、宾语和补语的位置，常常因其意义和组合关系变化而有所变化。例如：

◇ Did you know there have been only 14 people that have lived for more than 110 years?

你是否知道只有 14 位老人活了 110 多岁？（分句无宾语，谓前补后）

◇ Most bikes will last a lifetime.

大部分的自行车可以骑一辈子。（谓前补后）

━━━━━━ 练　　习 ━━━━━━

1. 翻译短文：

Now I am 80. Not a day's illness except a winter cough or twinge of arthritis. Today I still go fast up the four flights of steep stairs to my study in our tall houses, every day of the week, at nine o'clock in the morning, Saturdays and Sundays included, I groan at the work I have to do, cry out for leisure and think of this year's holiday. I don't stop writing until my wife calls me down to a delicious lunch. After an hour's nap, I do some household shopping, and return to take tea and then back to work at about four until seven, or in good weather go out and work in the garden. Unless we are going out we are in bed by 10. I sleep pretty well, dream wildly. I am not yet old enough to know loneliness.

2. 用"人"、"人们"或"人民"翻译下列句子：

(1) People want the foods which can keep their bodies healthy.

(2) Some people may feel that clever, successful people always make good use of advertisement.

(3) In this section you are going to hear extracts from an interview between two people.

(4) Today a great number of people travel from one country to another by plane.

(5) Normalization has opened new vistas among the peoples of the two countries.

(6) As I visited the Great Wall and the Summer Palace, I sensed the pride and the dignity which the Chinese legacy bestows upon the Chinese people.

(7) The book that you are going to read covers something about American people, some historical events, parties and their language.

3. 翻译下列带时量词语的句子:

(1) It must have been two hours since he left his comfortable house in the town.

(2) The old castle has stood on the little hill for over six hundred years.

(3) The climbers have been going up for some hours when the clouds covering the mountain peaks lifted for a moment.

(4) The old Dutch clock has been in the possession of the family for several generations.

(5) Some tired travelers, forced to spend a few hours in the town waiting for their train, were wandering aimlessly about.

(6) A disastrous fire broke out on the top floor of the hotel, but the flames were brought under control in two hours.

(7) The seaside town he planned to visit was about a three-hour train ride away.

Lesson 14
Literal Translation and Free Translation

直译(literal translation)和意译(free translation)是两种基本的翻译方法,既可以单独使用,也可以交叉使用,它们本身并没有哪个好哪个不好的问题。但是什么时候用哪一种方法,却很有讲究,选择不当会影响译文的质量。

所谓"直译",就是按照原文的意思和结构进行对译,译出来的话语或文字也符合目的语的表达习惯。例如:

◇ July can be very hot.

七月份可能很热。

◇ The local supermarket saved me.

当地的超市救了我。

◇ It is called *chanoyu*.

这叫"茶道"。

◇ But the matter is not as simple as that.

但是事情并不那么简单。

◇ Three things seem to be very important: fresh air, fresh food and a simple way of life.

三件事看来很重要:新鲜空气、新鲜食品和简朴的生活方式。

但是,直译不等于逐字逐句地机械死译,也不是脱离原文精神实质的生搬硬套。在英译汉中,只有在英语句子所表达的内容和方式与相应的汉语句子一致或者接近的情况下,才可以用直译法。虽然这是一种简便的方法,可是如果把不能直译的句子硬译成汉语,一字不多,一字不少,一词不先,一词不后,那就是死译,别人无法看懂。下面是一些典型的死译:

◇ Cycling is good for you.

＊骑自行车是好为了你。

◇ Others choose to eat in the open air.

＊别的人选择吃在开放的空气。

这样的翻译语法不通,没有把原文的意思准确表达出来,无法进行交流。这是我们要力图避免的。

音译(transliteration)也是一种直译手段。

一般来说,单词、短语、部分专有名词、术语、成语都有可能用直译法来翻译。

意译跟直译一样,都要求忠实于原文,但是在文字处理上可以不受句式、语序、词性、语态和标点符号的约束。为了更准确地表达原文的思想,可以在语法或修辞允许的范围内加减字数,调整语序,变换句式、词性或句子成分。如果说,直译法比较注重客观地传达原文内容的话,那么,意译法就更注重反映原文的文笔、风格和精神。例如:

◇ Today picnics are as popular as ever, ordinary family picnics or splendid
outdoor parties are held when the weather is good.

如今野餐比任何时候都更受欢迎。天公作美时既有寻常百姓家的野餐,
也有丰盛的户外聚餐。 (调整语序,增加词语)

虽然意译有较大的灵活性,但是也受原文的内容和风格,以及目的语的语法、修辞、表达习惯等规则的限制。随心所欲地改变原文的意思,不必要地添枝加叶,盲目地改换句子结构,在意译中都是不允许的。

意译在文学作品的翻译中使用很广。意译和直译在实际翻译中常常交叉使用,相互配合,缺一不可。

◎ 思 考 题 ◎

1. 直译的含义是什么?请说明它的意义和使用范围。
2. 举例说明音译的类别和作用。使用这种翻译方法时应该注意什么问题?
3. 意译的含义是什么?使用意译法时应该考虑哪些因素?
4. 如何认识直译和意译两者之间的互补作用?

练 习

翻译下面的句子并说明所使用的译法。

(1) I can't touch anything sweet. It's my teeth.

(2) No one knows for sure how people first learned to preserve food.

(3) Trucks, trains, planes and refrigerator ships are modern ways of transporting
food.

(4) My, what a downpour! And there's no sign of its stopping.

(5) September and October were nicest months, but November was terrible. We
had a lot of rain.

(6) Are you being served, sir? What can we do for you here?

(7) I'd like to make an appointment to see Mr. Smith tomorrow if I may.

(8) I just dropped in to say hello.

(9) I've noticed that books in the library are listed under three headings: author, title and subject.

(10) Our world is getting smaller and smaller. Scientists hope to find enough mineral, vegetable and animal wealth in the sea to provide food for the entire world.

Lesson 15
Drinking and Driving

The legal limit for driving after drinking alcohol is 80 milligrams of alcohol in 100 millilitres of blood, when tested.① But there is no sure way of telling how much you can drink before you reach this limit. It varies with each person depending on your weight, your sex②, if you've just eaten and what sort of drinks you've had.

In fact, your driving ability can be affected by just one or two drinks. You could be taken to a police station if your driving has been affected by alcohol. It takes about an hour for the body to get rid of the alcohol in one standard drink. So, if you have a heavy drinking session in the evening③ you might find that your driving is still affected the next morning. The only way to be sure you are safe is not to drink at all.

Alcohol is a major cause of road traffic accidents. One in three of the drivers killed in road accidents have levels of alcohol which are over the legal limit④, and road accidents after drinking are the biggest cause of death among young men.

It is important to remember that driving after you've been drinking doesn't just affect you. If you are involved in an accident it affects a lot of other people as well, not least the person you might kill or injure.

● 注　　释 ●

① The legal limit for driving after drinking alcohol is 80 milligrams of alcohol in 100 millilitres of blood, when tested.
按照法律规定,酒后开车的血液酒精含量检查时每 100 毫升不得超过 80 毫克。

② It varies with each person depending on your weight, your sex.
它因人而异,取决于你的体重和性别。

③ if you have a heavy drinking session in the evening
如果你晚间狂饮过

④ One in three of the drivers killed in road accidents have levels of alcohol which are over the legal limit.

三分之一死于交通事故的驾车人酒精都超出法定限量。

※ 译词分析 ※

"with"的翻译

英语介词的搭配力强,与不同的介词、动词和名词组合可构成各类短语,充当句子成分,用来表示特定的意思和语法关系。一般来说,英语介词可以译成汉语的介词。但是因为现代汉语的不少介词都源于动词,所以也常用动词或动词短语来对译。

1. 把"with"译为"跟":

◇ My wife is here with me.

我太太跟我在一起。

2. 把"with"译为"用":

◇ New-born babies can grasp objects with either of their hands.

新生婴儿可以用任何一只手抓东西。

◇ The Greeks and the Romans made music by plucking strings with their fingers.

希腊人和罗马人用手指拨动琴弦演奏乐曲。

3. "with"译为"着":

◇ In Tibet a cup of tea is served with a lump of yak butter floating on its surface.

在西藏,一杯茶端上来时表面上总是浮着一块酥油。

◇ The roads were covered with slippery ice or deep snow.

路上覆盖着滑滑的冰或厚厚的雪。

4. 把"with"译为"有":

◇ Before the night each guest receives a menu with a number against one dish.

头一天晚上每一位客人都得到一张菜名旁边标有号码的菜单。

◇ Pies and sausages with Protena in them will be served in schools, hospitals and works canteens.

掺有普罗特那的馅饼和香肠将供应学校、医院和工厂的餐室。

5. "with"可与某些动词结合构成固定搭配,也可与名词或复合结构结合构成短语作状语。这些短语有多种译法,需根据具体意思选择译词。如:

◇ I suggested going on with the match later.

我建议以后再继续进行比赛。

◇ It varies with each person depending on your weight and sex.

它因人而异,取决于你的体重和性别。

◇ Then paths are covered with fallen leaves.

小路上铺满了落叶。

◇ She couldn't compete with prices.

她在价格上无法跟人竞争。

◇ The Russians usually take lump sugar with their tea.

俄国人一般都在茶里加方糖。

1. 翻译短文:

Drive carefully when pedestrians are about, particularly in crowded shopping streets. Drive slowly near schools, and look out for children getting on or off school buses. Three out of four pedestrians killed or seriously injured are either under fifteen or over sixty. The young and the elderly may not judge speeds very well, and may step into the road when you do not expect them. Give them, and infirm, or blind, or disabled people, plenty of time to cross the road.

2. 翻译下面带定语从句的句子:

(1) The news bulletin that we heard a few moments ago said that the doctor was making every effort to save the child.

(2) The village he lives in is a beauty-spot.

(3) The longest walk that I ever went was over 20 miles.

(4) These are the pictures that they were laughing at.

(5) The skirt that I gave my sister for her birthday is already worn out.

(6) The glass that you are drinking out of hasn't been washed.

3. 翻译下列句子,注意介词"with"的不同译法。

(1) Two of his brothers died of tuberculosis. Then he became ill with the same disease.

(2) Some female deer were grazing in a field with their fawns.

(3) Looking round, he realized with a shock that he was the only passenger left on the bus.

(4) She was busy mixing butter and flour and her hands were soon covered with sticky pastry.

(5) A black car with four men inside stopped at the gate.

(6) They noticed with dismay that the train was coming towards them at tremendous speed.

(7) Although working in different provinces they keep in touch with one another.

4. 完成下面句子的翻译：

(1) His ideas were too strange to please the men who hired him.

他的想法很奇怪,_____。

(2) The man who felt he should have died at birth is remembered and respected long after death.

_____在他去世很久之后还一直受到人们的怀念和尊敬。

(3) Nowadays young couples have to give serious thought to the number of children they want, can afford, or can raise successfully.

如今对于_____青年夫妇得认真加以考虑。

(4) He joined a group of other fliers who had traveled around the country and would give demonstrations of their skill.

他加入了飞行员的行列,_____。

(5) He is admired for both the physical courage which brought him fame and his ability to resist the temptation to profit.

人们钦佩_____,也赞美_____。

(6) Most children obtain their education in government schools where tuition is free at primary and secondary levels.

多数儿童在公立学校接受教育,_____。

Lesson 16
Flying over the Pole

We all know that it is possible for ordinary people to make their homes on the equator, although often they feel uncomfortably hot there.[①] Millions do it. But as for the North Pole — we know that it is not only a dangerously cold place, but that people like you and me would find it quite impossible to live there. At the present time, only scientists and explorers can do so, and they use special equipment. Men have been traveling across and around the equator on wheels, on their feet or in ships for thousands of years[②]; but only a few men, with great difficulty and in very recent times have ever crossed the ice to the North Pole.

So it may surprise you to learn that, when traveling by air, it is really safer to fly over the North Pole than over the equator.[③] Of course, this is not true about landings in the polar region (which passenger aeroplanes do not make), but the weather, if we are flying at a height of 5,000 metres above the Pole, is a delight. At 4,000 metres and more above the earth you can always be sure that there will not be a cloud in the sky as far as the eye can see. In the tropics, on the other hand, you are not certain to keep clear of bad weather even at such heights as 18,000 or 20,000 metres.[④]

Aeroplanes can't climb as high or as quickly in cold air as in warm air. Nor can clouds. In practice, this is an advantage to the aeroplane, which is already at a good height when it reaches the polar region and so does not need to climb, while at the same time cold air keeps the clouds down low.[⑤]

● 注　　释 ●

① it is possible for ordinary people to make their homes on the equator, although often they feel uncomfortably hot there.

虽然普通人在赤道地区往往会感到炎热难当,但是在那儿安家还是可能的。

② Men have been traveling across and around the equator on wheels, on their feet or in ships for thousands of years.

几千年来不断有人坐车、步行或者乘船穿越赤道,或者环绕赤道旅行。

③ when traveling by air, it is really safer to fly over the North Pole than over the equator.

乘飞机飞越北极确实比飞越赤道更安全。

④ you are not certain to keep clear of bad weather even at such heights as 18,000 or 20,000 metres.

即使飞到了 18000～20000 米,你也没有把握是否能避开恶劣的天气。

⑤ while at the same time cold air keeps the clouds down low.

而这时冷空气也阻止了云层上升。

※ 译法分析 ※

英语比较级的翻译

1. 英语表示比较级的句子多半带有英语形容词或副词的比较级或最高级以及"as...as"、"than"等。下面是几个表示比较的常见句型的翻译例句：

◇ Life would be easier if you lived at home.
   要是你呆在家里,日子总会过得舒坦些。

◇ Is it always as hot as in New Delhi?
   是不是总像新德里那样热?

◇ Some provinces have a longer winter and pratically no summer.
   有些省份冬天较长,实际上没有什么夏天。

◇ Nowadays it is much easier to walk than to drive.
   如今走路比开车容易得多。

2. 用于翻译否定比较级句子的汉语词语有"不如"、"不像"等。

◇ In the end her customers prefer to save money rather than have her friendly, personal service.
   最终她的顾客宁可省钱也不要她那友善而又亲切的服务。

◇ Aeroplanes can't climb as high or as quickly in cold air as in warm air.
   飞机在冷空气中不如在热空气中飞得高飞得快。

3. 常用于翻译英语形容词和副词最高级的汉语词语有:"最"、"……之一"和序数词等。例如:

◇ The most authoritative survey of the Nile was made by a Belgian in 1916.
   1916 年一个比利时人对尼罗河进行了最有权威的测量。

◇ Road accidents after drinking are the biggest cause of death.
   酒后开车发生的交通事故是造成死亡的最主要原因。

◇ The guitar is the most popular instrument in the world.
   吉他是世界上最流行的乐器。

4. 汉语比较意思的表达有时也可以通过上下文来体现,而不必借助于特定句式或具有比较意义的形容词和副词。例如:

◇ Gradually the weather gets milder and the snow begins to melt.

天气逐渐暖和起来,雪也开始融化了。

练　　习

1. 翻译短文:

Three British explorers, clad in wolfskins against the cold, rebuffed their critics early yesterday by reaching the South Pole seven weeks ahead of schedule in their attempt to make the first circumnavigation of the world on its polar axis. A radio message via New Zealand said that the British Transglobe Expedition got to the Pole at 4.35 a.m. It became only the third British party to achieve the feat, following Captain Scotain's fatal journey in 1912 and Vivian Fuch's expedition in 1958.

2. 翻译句子,注意英语比较方式的译法。

(1) The show was one of the dullest we have ever seen.

(2) Dolphins are more interesting than lions and tigers because they are livelier.

(3) Doctors have far less reason to worry about their health than other medical staff.

(4) These exercises are designed to teach what is presented in the lesson rather than to test student's knowledge.

(5) You are unable to enjoy your food unless you talk less at a dinner table.

(6) This hill is much lower than I thought it was.

(7) She is not so sophisticated as she makes herself out to be.

3. 多项选择(在与画线部分的意思一致的译文前的字母上画圈儿):

(1) In 1929 Byrd <u>successfully flew over the South Pole for the first time</u>.

    A. 为了头一回顺利地飞过南极　　　B. 第一次成功地飞越南极

    C. 为初次胜利地飞上南极　　　　　D. 首次赢了飞过南部的极

(2) Though at first, <u>Byrd and his men</u> were able to take a great many photos of the mountains below, they soon ran into serious trouble.

    A. 伯德和他的男人　　　　　　　　B. 伯德和部下们

    C. 伯德和伙计们　　　　　　　　　D. 伯德与人们

(3) <u>At one point</u>, it seemed certain that their plane would crash.

    A. 在一个点上　　　　　　　　　　B. 有一个地方

    C. 一个地点　　　　　　　　　　　D. 一点附近

(4) It could only <u>get over the mountains</u> if it rose to 10,000 feet.

    A. 克服山头   B. 爬过山头

    C. 飞过大山   D. 走上几座山

(5) Byrd at once ordered his men to throw out two heavy <u>food sacks</u>.

    A. 食品袋   B. 食品包裹

    C. 饮食粗布袋   D. 粮食硬纸袋

(6) The plane was then able to rise and it <u>cleared the mountains by 400 feet</u>.

    A. 从 400 英尺高清除大山   B. 按 400 英尺越过山

    C. 从距离山顶 400 英尺高度飞了过去   D. 用 400 英尺清除几座山

Lesson 17
Mock Meat

Up to thirty percent of artificial meat will be added to sausages, pies and tinned foods this year.[①]

A massive campaign to persuade butchers and food-processing firms to buy the "meat"—made from soya beans—was launched yesterday by the bakery company Rank Hovis McDougall[②].

They claim that their product, Protena, tastes, smells and looks just like meat. It costs up to twenty percent less than the real thing.

The firm hopes to sell two thousand tons of it this year. If they do, pies and sausages with Protena in them will be served in schools, hospitals and works canteens.

At a news conference yesterday Protena was added to all kinds of delicacies and offered to journalists to taste. Most noticed hardly any difference.[③]

Professor Alan Ward[④], Chairman of the Food Standards Committee, said yesterday: "Any food containing these items must be properly marked and labelled."

The committee has two years studying the use of soya products in food. Soya beans, which grow easily in hot climates, are now regarded as the food of the future.[⑤] They are much cheaper than meat to produce and provide just as much protein.

● 注　　释 ●

① Up to thirty percent of artificial meat will be added to sausages, pies and tinned foods this year.

今年掺入香肠、馅饼和罐头食品中的人造肉将高达 30%。

② the bakery company Rank Hovis McDougall

兰克·霍维斯·麦克杜格尔面包公司

③ Most noticed hardly any difference.

多数人几乎没有发现有什么不同。

④ Professor Alan Ward

艾伦·沃德教授

⑤ Soya beans, which grow easily in hot climates, are now regarded as the food of the future.

在炎热气候中易于种植的大豆,如今已被看做是未来的食品了。

※ 译 法 分 析 ※

英语动词加 ing 作定语的翻译

英语动词加 ing 单独放在名词前作定语,或者与名词、形容词、副词结合构成合成词放在名词前作定语,其语序跟汉语定语与中心语的位置相同,因此可以按顺序译出。例如:

◇ food-processing firm　　　食品加工公司
◇ traveling musicians　　　巡游乐师
◇ satisfying effect　　　令人满意的效果

英语动词的这种形式放在一个名词之后作修饰短语时,其意义相当于一个定语从句。如果把它译成一个简短的汉语定语的话必须放在中心语之前。例如:

◇ Any food containing these items must be properly marked and labelled.

含这些配料的任何食品都应当确切标明并贴上标记。

1. 翻译短文:

The British often get their meals ready very quickly. Many wives go out to work, so they do not have time to spend in the kitchen. In supermarkets there are a lot of tins and packets. The housewife only has to open a tin or a packet, cook the food for a few minutes, and the meal is ready. On Sunday, there is usually a bigger, better lunch. It is often a big piece of roast meat with potatoes and green vegetables; and after that, pudding.

2. 翻译下列句子,注意英语动词带 ing 形式的译法。

(1) The baobab is a strange-looking tree, but it is extremely useful.

(2) Nylon can be used as insulating cover on electric wire.

(3) A skunk often defends itself by giving a warning signal and spraying a terrible-smelling substance.

(4) Motorists going north were advised to use Highway No. 316.

(5) People straggling to higher ground were just in time to escape the ravages of the flood.

(6) Like many bachelors approaching middle age, he was getting rather set in his ways.

(7) Few students entering these classes have much experience in writing composition in Chinese without guidance.

3. 用所提示的词语翻译下列句子：

(1) Pupils preparing for the entrance examination should read this book.

（准备参加入学考试）

(2) Each lesson in the book contains a text giving examples of Chinese grammar and characters. （举出汉语语法和汉字的例子）

(3) The museum is filled with objects dating from different historical periods.

（标明不同历史时期）

(4) Now, in spite of their size, whales are no longer an even match for men using helicopters, radar and harpoons. （拥有直升飞机、雷达和鱼叉装备）

(5) Stories of dolphins helping drowning sailors have been common since Roman times. （救助溺水水手）

(6) We are not surprised when we read about a politician having talks with the Japanese Prime Minister one day, attending a conference in Australia the following morning.

（第一天与日本首相举行会谈,第二天上午在澳大利亚参加一次会议）

(7) Television companies receive a large number of letters every week complaining about programmes with adult themes being shown at times when young children may be awake.

（抱怨在年幼的子女可能还没睡觉时就播放成年人题材的节目）

Lesson 18
Patient Knows Best

A person's answer to the question "Is your health excellent, good, fair or poor?" is a remarkable predictor of who will live or die over the next four years[1], according to new findings.

A study of more than 2800 men and women aged 65 and older found that those who rate their health "poor" are four to five times more likely to die in the next four years than those who rate their health "excellent".[2] This was the case even if examinations show the respondents to be in comparable health.

These findings are supported by a review of five other large studies, totaling 23,000 people, which reached similar conclusions, according to Ellen Idler, a sociologist at Rutgers University[3], and epidemiologist Stanislav Kasl of Yale University School of Medicine[4], co-authors of the new study.

There are several ways in which a person's feelings may be a good indicator of his or her underlying health. Experts believe people take into account not only their own susceptibility to illness, exhaustion level and mood[5], but such things as their parents' and siblings' health histories — all of which may greatly influence the person who becomes ill. Being optimistic may also have its own positive effect[6].

(By Daniel Goleman)

● 注　　释 ●

① is a remarkable predictor of who will live or die over the next four years
能对今后四年之内是否健在或死亡做出惊人的预测

② those who rate their health "poor" are four to five times more likely to die in the next four years than those who rate their health "excellent".
那些把自己的健康情况列为"差"的人在今后四年之内死亡的可能性,是那些把自己的健康情况列为"佳"的人的 4～5 倍。

③ Ellen Idler, a sociologist at Rutgers University
拉特格斯大学的社会学家埃伦·伊德拉

④ epidemiologist Stanislav Kasl of Yale University School of Medicine

耶鲁大学医学院的流行病学家斯坦尼斯拉夫·卡斯尔

⑤ susceptibility to illness, exhaustion level and mood

容易染病、疲劳程度和情绪波动

⑥ positive effect

积极作用

※ 译法分析 ※

英语一般过去时的翻译

汉语语法没有时态系统,词汇没有严格意义的形态变化,因此翻译英语一般过去时主要靠词汇手段。具体的方法是:

1. 使用时间词语如"以前"、"古代"、"早先"、"去年"、"那时"等;

2. 使用作状语的副词如"已经"、"曾经"、"刚才"、"一度"等;

3. 使用动词尾缀"过"或"了";

4. 使用结构"自从……以来";

5. 通过上下文来体现。请看下面的例子:

◇ It started to rain half-way through the game and I couldn't stand playing in the rain.

比赛才进行一半就下起了雨,挨着雨淋打球真受不了。

◇ In 1969 some scientists remeasured the length of the river and found it to be 6,712 km long.

1969 年一些科学家再次对那条河进行了测量,发现其长度为 6,712 公里。

◇ This was the case even if examinations show the respondents to be in comparable health.

即使检查表明回答者是处于比较健康状态,事实也是如此。

练 习

1. 翻译短文:

One day at the office of the orthopedic specialist I work for, we had to make arrangements for an elderly patient with spinal arthritis to have a special injection. We said we would phone him with the information. Two days later, the patient called us, concerned that he had missed our call because of his poor hearing. "I can barely hear, barely see and barely walk," he told me. Then he added cheerfully, "Things

60

could be worse, though. At least I can still drive."

2. 翻译下列句子,注意汉语表达过去行为和事情的方式。

(1) I didn't tell you anything that wasn't true.

(2) I wonder why they didn't ring him up direct.

(3) Each year they bought something new to wear.

(4) I wanted to be sure you had everything you wanted.

(5) She couldn't sleep herself much at night, so she didn't want to let me sleep.

(6) A disastrous fire broke out on the top floor of the hotel in the morning.

(7) My father always swore that he would never have a TV set in the house.

(8) Before the war, when wages were relatively low, people did not think of buying luxuries for themselves.

3. 下面的句子可以连接成一段话,原文主要靠时态来表示事情发生在过去。翻译成汉语时注意上下文和背景成分的表达,使读者感觉到那是一段往事。

(1) They had a very good time when they were away.

(2) The sun was out nearly all the time, and the sea looked beautiful.

(3) There were nice people staying in the hotel.

(4) When the day came on which they had to leave they were sorry to go.

(5) The taxi was at the door to take them to the station when one of them could not find his hat.

(6) They didn't want to miss the train, so the man left the hotel without his hat.

Lesson 19
Civilization in the New Century

One scientist believes that marriage will be meaningless, because reproductive banks will help produce human babies.[①] Another asserts that direct mind-to-mind communication will replace phone calls and faxes. Similarly, switches may disappear one day, as lights and machines can be turned on and off mentally.

Such progress has already been partially made. Kevin Warwick[②], a professor of cybernetics, is reported to have implanted a chip in his arm to control the computer and door in his office. Both he and his wife wish to find out if an implanted chip can help them to read mutual minds without any talking.[③]

But a good number of scholars have seen the gloomy side of the picture. They think that it will be terrible if humans who become frustrated and unimaginative individuals live in a restless society. The American linguist Noam Chomsky[④] doubts if humans are "a kind of lethal mutation".

"A human brain is a stand-alone entity, guaranteeing a unique human identity[⑤]. But link a human brain with a machine, and what of the individual then?" Warwick writes in a book entitled *Prediction*.

● 注　释 ●

① because reproductive banks will help produce human babies.
因为繁殖库可以帮助人们生儿育女。

② Kevin Warwick
凯文·沃里克

③ an implanted chip can help them to read mutual minds without any talking.
植入的芯片能帮助他们不经交谈就可以知道彼此的心思。

④ Noam Chomsky
诺姆·乔姆斯基

⑤ guaranteeing a unique human identity
可以确保人类所具有的特性

※ 译法分析 ※

英语一般将来时的翻译

英语的一般将来时译为汉语时主要采用下列方法：

1. 用时间词语如"明天"、"明年"、"下月"、"下周"、"下一世纪"等；

2. 用作状语的副词如"将要"、"快要"、"要"、"会"等；

3. 使用结构"快要……了"和"就要……了"等；

4. 通过上下文来体现。

请看下面的例子：

◇ You'll get used to everything here in a year or two.

过一两年你对这里的一切都会习惯的。

◇ There'll be a new film at the Wudaokou Cinema.

五道口电影院要上映一部新电影。

◇ You will see that some of them will prefer to swing from their right hands and others will use their left hands.

你会看到有些猴子喜欢用右前肢荡秋千,而另外一些则用左前肢荡秋千。

◇ Up to thirty percent of artificial meat will be added to sausages, pies and tinned foods this year.

今年掺入香肠、馅饼和罐头食品的人造肉将高达 30%。

英语还可以用"be + going + 不定式"或"be + about + 不定式"来表示将要发生的动作和事情。这类句子译成汉语时方法同上。例如：

◇ They are going back to the bike.

他们将再次骑起自行车。

════════════════ 练　　习 ════════════════

1. 翻译短文：

As a Chinese student abroad, I am very much interested in the ongoing development of China. In the past, when my family mailed me a letter with a newspaper or a clipping enclosed, it took a week or ten days to reach me. Now I am glad to see that several Chinese newspapers have gone on line. I can read the news at the very same moment that it appears in China, thanks to the Internet. This is truly exciting for overseas students.

2. 翻译下列句子,注意汉语表达将来行为和事情的方式。

(1) Will the shops be open at 8 o'clock tomorrow morning?

(2) You'll always find a welcome here whenever you call.

(3) I shall try to persuade him to give up smoking before it is too late.

(4) I'll take the children to the zoo this afternoon if the weather is fine.

(5) The land they work on will not be fit for farming again for fifty years.

(6) We're a bit late for lunch, so if the dishes we want are now off the menu, we'll just have to take what's being served now.

3. 用所给词语翻译下列句子:

(1) They are going to put on another play soon.　　　　　　　　(将)

(2) What are we going to have for supper this evening?　　　　　(打算)

(3) We are going to have the room painted white sometime next week.　　(要)

(4) When are you going to have your bathwater turned on?　　　　(想)

(5) Is your sister going to make any more cakes like these?　　　(还)

(6) Tom, you are going to do the washing tomorrow!　　　　　　(得)

(7) You are going to have an early breakfast, I promise.　　　(早一点)

Lesson 20
Online Service

Are you web surfers or online chatters?[1] Have you ever sent e-mail messages to your friends? How much do you know about multimedia or online shopping, job hunting, visa application services? Nowadays computers are so important in our daily life that we cannot live without them. While rendering tremendous assistance to those in need, believe or not, they can also make a great trouble. The following are true stories:

The Raytheon Corporation in Massachusetts sued 21 online chatters who were believed to be[2] its employees disclosing company secrets.

A Canadian was arrested after his death threats against the American president had been made over the Internet. The police also impounded his computer equipment and software.[3]

The U. S. Vice President Albert Gore helped lead the federal response to the Y2K computer threat, but his computer bug took a tiny bite out of the website[4] he had established for his campaign to become president.

February 29 was a leap day for the year 2000 on which any computer technology problem was possible to occur. Experts around the world geared up for trouble shooting. About 150 Americans staffed two shifts a day from February 28 to March 1 at the Information Coordination Centre.[5] Their job was to compile data on any errors in key systems across the U. S. They stayed in touch with the steering committee of the International Y2K Cooperation Centre funded by the World Bank.

● 注　　释 ●

① Are you web surfers or online chatters?

你是网上冲浪者还是网上侃爷?

② The Raytheon Corporation in Massachusetts sued 21 online chatters who were believed to be ....

马萨诸塞州的雷锡昂公司控告了 21 名网上侃爷,据信他们是……。

③ The police also impounded his computer equipment and software.

警方还没收了他的电脑设备和软件。

④ Albert Gore helped lead the federal response to the Y2K computer threat, but his computer bug took a tiny bite out of the website....

艾伯特·戈尔曾领导联邦政府对付新千年的电脑威胁,但是他的网址却被自己的电脑的千年虫咬了一小口……。

⑤ About 150 Americans staffed two shifts a day from February 28 to March 1 at the Information Coordination Centre.

从 2 月 28 日至 3 月 1 日大约 150 个美国人每天两班倒,在信息协调中心工作。

※ 译法分析 ※

英语现在完成体的翻译

英语的现在完成体由“have”的人称形式和谓语动词的过去分词来表达,常与“already”、“yet”或“since”呼应。汉语的现在完成体主要由谓语动词后的助词“了”来表示,常与“已经”或“曾经”一类副词配合。某些汉语结果补语如“完”、“好”、“过”、“掉”或“成”也可用来表示完成意义。翻译英语现在完成体的句子时除上述词语外还常用“还”、“刚”、“一直”、“到现在”或“自从”等词语。例如:

◇ Since then Lake Nasser has been filled up.

从那以后纳赛尔湖已蓄满了水。

◇ People are looking for cheaper kinds of transport, and they have found one from the past.

人们正在寻找各种经济实惠的交通工具,并且已经从过去的交通工具中找到了一种。

◇ Have you ever sent e-mail messages to your friends?

你是否曾经给朋友发过电子邮件?

练　习

1. 翻译短文:

The U.S. embassy in Beijing has begun a drop-off visa application system for Chinese travelers who have received visas and visited the country within the past five years. Applicants eligible for this service can simply drop off their application at any CITIC Industrial Bank (中信银行) branch in Beijing where they can pay their fee. Visas can then be picked up at the same branch four working days later. An updated list of participating bank branches is available on the embassy's web page.

2. 翻译下列句子,注意汉语完成体的表达方式。

(1) What good books have you read during the last few months?

(2) Have you written down all the questions that we must answer?

(3) Has she ever eaten mangoes? Shall we add the fruit to our shopping list?

(4) Don't frighten the child by taking him to the reptile show. He's never seen a snake.

(5) My granny has lived in the old house since her marriage with my grandpa.

(6) I've just rung Alison but she didn't answer. She must be away from home.

(7) I'm going to make a Chinese dish for our guests. I've made it before from time to time.

3. 完成下列句子的翻译:

(1) As you can see, we have just moved into our new house.

你们看得出来,_____。

(2) It's rather short notice for you, but I've just received an e-mail from my girl friend about her coming.

没能早点告诉你们,_____。

(3) When the operation has been done the patient will feel better.

_____病人就会觉得好一些。

(4) We received your letter last week at our old address but I haven't had time to answer it until now.

上星期我们在原来住处接到了你寄来的信,_____。

(5) I'm afraid the job I've got for you won't be easy.

_____恐怕不那么轻松。

(6) I've run up against all kinds of people, working as a temporary.

作为一个临时工_____。

(7) The only trouble I've ever had was with someone who wasn't interested in my typing.

_____对我打的字不喜欢的人。

Lesson 21
New Year's Day

The last day of the year, known in England as New Year's Eve, has a different name in Scotland. There it is called *Hogmanay*. To Scotsmen *Hogmanay* is a word that conjures up many pleasant associations: good whisky and first footers, to name only a few.[①]

Auld Lang Syne[②] is the traditional song which has been sung at midnight on New Year's Eve since the beginning of the 18th century. It is famous now throughout the English-speaking world. As for "first footers", ideally from a Scottish point of view they are tall dark strangers who bear a piece of coal and a sprig of mistletoe.[③] They appear at the door after midnight and are supposed to bring good luck.

Welcoming the new year is one of the oldest customs celebrated the world over. In many places people stay up late to watch the old year out and the new year in.[④] Almost everywhere in the world church bells ring, horns toot, whistles blow, sirens shriek.[⑤] The hulabaloo expresses people's high spirits at holiday time. Many years ago, however, the loud noises were meant to scare away the evil spirits.

New Year's Day is a time for entertaining, visiting, and in many places, gift-giving.

The idea of a "clean start" for the new year means exactly that in many places. In part of the Balkans[⑥], the people sprinkle themselves with freshly drawn well water. People in Morocco observe the same practice. The people in Madagascar and Myanmar pour water on their heads on New Year's Day.

● 注　　释 ●

① *Hogmanay* is a word that conjures up many pleasant associations: good whisky and first footers, to name only a few.
"霍格马内"这个词会使人产生许多愉快的联想,随便举几个例子来说:美酒威士忌和第一批来访者。

② *Auld Lang Syne*

《美好的往日》(又译为《愿友谊地久天长》)

③ As for "first footers", ideally from a Scottish point of view they are tall dark strangers who bear a piece of coal and a sprig of mistletoe.

至于"第一批来访者",从苏格兰人的观点看来最好是一些个儿高、皮肤黑的陌生人,各人手里拿着一块煤和一枝槲寄生。

④ In many places people stay up late to watch the old year out and the new year in.

在许多地方人们都熬夜守岁,辞旧迎新。

⑤ church bells ring, horns toot, whistles blow, sirens shriek.

教堂的钟声回响,号角齐鸣,哨笛长啸。

⑥ England　　　　英格兰

　　Scotland　　　苏格兰

　　the Balkans　　巴尔干半岛各国

　　Morocco　　　 摩洛哥

　　Madagascar　　马达加斯加

　　Myanmar　　　缅甸

※ 译法分析 ※

汉语四字格在翻译中的运用

汉语中有许多"四字格"(由四个汉字按一定规则组成的)成语,形式简洁,语义精辟,结构凝练,音节和谐。其中许多出自于古今群众的口头语言,也有一部分来源于中国古代寓言故事或其他文学作品,还有不少是由历史事件凝缩而成的。

英译汉中恰当地使用四字格成语,可以使译文简洁生动,几个字就可以表达复杂丰富的内容,达到比喻、形容、夸张、委婉或双关的修辞效果。此外,它还可以增强译文的节奏感,产生和谐与对称的语言美。四字格成语虽然在书面语中用得较多,但是有不少在日常口语中也常常使用。只要英文的意思与汉语成语的意思相同或者接近,语体和语用功能符合,我们就可以酌情使用。例如:

◇ The sky is blue.　　　　　　　　　　　碧空如洗

◇ cloudless　　　　　　　　　　　　　　万里无云

◇ can do nothing about it　　　　　　　　无能为力

◇ (a businessman's) dream　　　　　　　梦寐以求

◇ can be fun　　　　　　　　　　　　　其乐无穷

◇ we all know　　　　　　　　　　　　众所周知

◇ produce human babies　　　　　　　　生儿育女

◇ rendering tremendous assistance to those in need 　　患难之交
◇ watch the old year out and the new year in 　　辞旧迎新

在翻译中也可以使用一些由四个汉字组成的词组。这些词组虽然不是成语,但具有四字格成语的相同特点,因而会产生相同的修辞和表达效果。例如:

◇ oily（hair） 　　油光锃亮
◇ look funny 　　滑稽可笑
◇ be warm all the year round 　　四季如春
◇ black clouds cover the sky 　　乌云密布
◇ a heavy fall of rain 　　大雨倾盆
◇ cheap 　　经济实惠
◇ last a lifetime 　　毕生受用
◇ a healthy old age 　　健康长寿
◇ uncomfortably hot 　　炎热难当
◇ people like you and me 　　你我之辈
◇ Church bells ring, horns toot, whistles blow, sirens shriek.

　　　　　　　教堂的钟声回响,号角齐鸣,哨笛长啸。

━━━━━━ 练　　习 ━━━━━━

1. 翻译短文:

February 14th is known as St. Valentine's Day throughout Europe and North America. It is customary to send a card bearing an affectionate message to someone you admire. You are not supposed to sign your name, and part of the fun is trying to guess who has sent the card. In the Midddle Ages February 14th was also the day when birds were thought to pair off. Evidently it was considered a good idea for humans to select their mates on the same day. In modern times St. Valentine's Day is big business. The manufacturers of cards and gifts are grateful for the continuation of the old custom.

2. 用所给词语完成下列句子的翻译:

(1) If you are really down, even little tasks can seem large.
如果你真的情绪低落,＿＿＿＿＿＿＿＿＿＿＿＿＿＿＿＿＿。（鸡毛蒜皮）

(2) This is why leaves appear dizzyingly bright and clear on a sunny fall day.
这就是为什么在阳光灿烂的秋日＿＿＿＿＿＿＿＿＿＿＿＿＿＿＿。
（光彩夺目）

(3) I'd heard delays occur when the weather gets bad.

我听说_____就总会有晚点的事。（天不作美）

(4) Outside torrential rains are threatening to sweep my little house off the mountain slope on which it teeters.

外面大雨如注，仿佛要_____。（摇摇欲坠）

(5) A car goes by, the driver and passenger staring at the well-dressed foreigner walking backward and holding his thumb out in the downpour.

一辆汽车开了过去，司机和乘客都注视着那个穿戴讲究的外国人_____。（倾盆大雨）

(6) Flooded with calls, the company is maximizing profits by handling only in-city runs.

_____，出租汽车公司只安排市内运营就可以大捞一把。（应接不暇）

(7) To get me to my plane, he has abandoned his post and raced from the company in his personal car.

为了送我去赶航班，_____。（马不停蹄）

3. 选择恰当的汉语四字格翻译下列句子：

(1) The bright young kid never took himself seriously.

(2) Her thin eyebrows above her sharp eyes gave her a delicate look.

(3) He looked at the picture without much interest.

(4) The man of about fifty has a merry face and dark hair.

(5) She stared at him in a sleepy, steady way, indifferent but rather cautious.

(6) When they called for their friend nobody answered the door.

(7) The stranger came in and his eyes wandered everywhere.

Lesson 22
Chinese Cooking

Eating anywhere in China can be such a zesty, tasty experience that words do no justice.① Today a group of British gourmets are leaving from Gatwick on a direct flight to Beijing for a 20-day tour of Chinese cuisine enjoyment organized by *The Observer*. In each city they visit they will attempt not only to taste the characteristic dishes there, but also to eat at one of the best local restaurants.

They understand that there are the Cantonese, Fujianese, Hunan, Shandong, Sichuan, Jiangsu and Yangzhou styles of cooking② in China. They will begin their tasting by having a 17-course royal-styled banquet in Beijing.

The party will go to Sichuan by train. The province is blessed with good rice, bamboo, wheat, corn, fruits of all sorts. The Sichuan people believe in extremes: very sour, very hot, sweet or salty, with their own regional salt, pepper, star anise and coriander. They don't like Cantonese stir-frying, but prefer steaming and simmering.③

They will then fly from Chengdu to Hangzhou — the home of many wonderful dishes which shouldn't be missed. The "beggars' chicken"④ is prepared by covering it with special clay and stuffing it with lotus seeds. The shrimp and rice crust is fine, as is a stewed pork named for the poet Su Dongpo. Suzhou is nearby, but has totally different specialities.

From Hangzhou they will fly to Guangzhou where the food is the most exotic and varied in all China. There isn't much long broiling or barbecueing as in the north, nor simmering for hours with spices and herbs as in the west. The local people steam fish and stir-fry their vegetables.⑤ And as for meats, they roast them. One of their barbecued dishes, the pork, is beautifully reddish on the outside, while white and juicy inside.

The weather should be perfect, especially for their appetite. The tour that they are making is believed to be the first and the best of its kind ever organized.

● 注　　释 ●

① Eating anywhere in China can be such a zesty, tasty experience that words do no

72

justice.

在中国任何地方吃饭都是一种口齿留香的体验,无法用语言来表达。

② the Cantonese, Fujianese, Hunan, Shandong, Sichuan, Jiangsu and Yangzhou styles of cooking

广东菜、福建菜、湖南菜、山东菜、四川菜、江苏菜和扬州菜

③ They don't like Cantonese stir-frying, but prefer steaming and simmering.

他们不喜欢广东式的炒菜,而喜欢蒸和炖。

④ The "beggars' chicken"   叫花子鸡

The shrimp and rice crust   虾仁锅巴

a stewed pork named for the poet Su Dongpo   东坡肉

⑤ The local people steam fish and stir-fry their vegetables.

当地人做清蒸鱼,炒青菜。

※ 译法分析 ※

英语现在进行时的翻译

英语的"现在进行时"由助动词 be 的人称形式与相关动词的现在分词构成。汉语的进行体常用助词"着"、副词或副词性结构"正(在)"、"一直"、"不断"、"不停"、"(正)在……呢"等来表示。例如:

◇ Today a group of British gourmets are leaving from Gatwick on a direct flight to Beijing for a 20-day tour of Chinese cuisine enjoyment organized by *The Observer*.

今天一批英国美食家正从盖特威克机场直飞北京,进行由《观察家报》组织的为期 20 天品尝中国菜的访问。

汉语表现动作进行有时也可以通过上下文来体现,而不必用"着"或"正在"之类的词语,例如:

◇ You're talking about last winter in Beijing.

你说的是北京去年冬天的情况。

◇ The tour they are making is believed to be the first and the best of its kind ever organized.

据信他们的中国之行是所组织的这类访问中的第一次,也将是最成功的一次。

1. 翻译短文:

The Chinese are as good at cooking as are the French, and they go to immense trouble to see that dishes are properly prepared and served. An old saying lays it down that every dish should delight by its appearance and smell as well as by its taste. Festivals, birthdays or marriages are usually celebrated with a meal of at least a dozen courses, often eaten in a restaurant, with the guests seated at round tables and using chopsticks. There are many thousands of recipes. Almost every Chinese province has its own style of preparing food, but basically the method is the same.

2. 翻译下列句子,注意汉语进行体的表达方式。

(1) My nephew is cooking in the kitchen now.

(2) Now we are living in the countryside 20 kilometres away from our old house.

(3) Why are you laughing at me? Have I made any mistake?

(4) It's raining heavily. Take an umbrella with you.

(5) The kids are watching television in the room. They've done their homework.

(6) They want to find out what is happening outside?

(7) She is working so attentively that she forgets the kettle is boiling.

3. 完成下列句子的翻译:

(1) What I'm really looking for is an advanced Chinese course, three or four hours a day, leaving the afternoons free.

_____,每天三四个小时,下午不上课。

(2) I'm sending you an enrolment form. Please complete and post it off before this weekend.

_____,请填好并在周末前寄出。

(3) The exhibition hall is in the process of decoration and rearrangement.

展览大厅_____。

(4) She is having kittens because her husband has not come back yet.

_____因为她丈夫还没回家。

(5) The kids are making terrible noise. Will you please take them away?

_____,请把他们带走吧。

(6) I'm enclosing a curriculum vitae, together with references from two companies I have worked for.

_____以及我曾任职的两个公司的证明信。

(7) I am writing to you to express my dissatisfaction with the service offered by your company on a recent flight from New York to Beijing.

_____,表达我对贵公司在纽约至北京最近一次航班上所提供的服务的不满。

Lesson 23
The Great Wall

The sights of Beijing are so numerous that one can spend several weeks here and leave without having seen all of the important ones.① The Summer Palace would probably head any list of attractions, with perhaps the Temple of Heaven coming second. In addition to these places inside the city, there are many others outside: the Great Wall, the Ming Tombs, the Western Hills and so on.

A trip from the city to Badaling can be made in less than two hours. For centuries the Great Wall which has fired the imagination of men surpasses all other physical human undertakings.② The construction of the wall began in the seventh century B.C. when separate feudal states in northern China built barriers against invasions by neighbouring states along their borders. In the third century B.C. the great Emperor Shi Huangdi of the Qin Dynasty③ ordered the separate sections of the walls linked together to form the basis of the present Great Wall. Beginning at Shanhaiguan Pass at Bohai Bay in the east end, the wall rises and falls through Shaanxi Province, twists and turns along the Yellow River and comes to an end at Jiayuguan Pass in Gansu Province.④ An Englishman who saw the Great Wall in 1790 estimated that it contained more brick and stone than were to be found in the United Kingdom; and a later visitor said that the material employed was sufficient to build a wall eight feet high and three feet thick that would encircle the globe at the equator.⑤

The wall traverses plains and mountains being at some points 1,300 metres above sea level. The wall averaged 7.8 metres in height and 5.8 metres in width at the top. At intervals of 1,500 to 2,000 metres throughout the length of the wall there are defense towers which are about 3 metres higher than the wall itself.

The Great Wall remains today as it has been for more than twenty centuries the only work of man that is visible from the moon.⑥

● 注　　释 ●

① one can spend several weeks here and leave without having seen all of the important ones.

一个人就是在这儿呆上几个星期，离开时也许没能把主要的景点看完。

② the Great Wall which has fired the imagination of men surpasses all other physical human undertakings.

激发人们想像力的长城超越了所有其他人工工程。

③ the great Emperor Shi Huangdi of the Qin Dynasty　　秦始皇

④ Shanhaiguan Pass　　　　　　　　　　　　　　　　山海关

　　Bohai Bay　　　　　　　　　　　　　　　　　　　渤海湾

　　Shaanxi Province　　　　　　　　　　　　　　　　陕西

　　the Yellow River　　　　　　　　　　　　　　　　黄河

　　Jiayuguan Pass　　　　　　　　　　　　　　　　　嘉峪关

　　Gansu Province　　　　　　　　　　　　　　　　　甘肃省

⑤ the material employed was sufficient to build a wall eight feet high and three feet thick that would encircle the globe at the equator.

长城所使用的材料足以建筑一堵 8 英尺高 3 英尺厚的墙沿着赤道绕地球一周。

⑥ The Great Wall remains today…the only work of man that is visible from the moon.

长城……是从月球上可以看到的惟一人工建筑。

※ 译法分析 ※

英语句子主语的翻译

1. 英语的名词、代词、数词和名词化的其他词语都可以作句子的主语，这与汉语名词、代词、数量词作主语的情况基本是一致的。这样的句子多半可以直接译出。例如：

　　◇ The wall traverses plains and mountains being at some points 1,300 metres above sea level.

　　　长城跨越平原高山，在某些地方海拔 1,300 米。

　　◇ They take their lunch or tea out into the countryside and have a picnic.

　　　他们把午饭或茶点带到乡下去野餐。

　　◇ Cycling is clean, quiet, cheap and healthy.

　　　骑车很干净、安静、经济，有益于健康。

　　◇ Millions do it.

　　　千百万人都这样做。

　　◇ February 29 was a leap day for the year 2000.

　　　2000 年 2 月 29 日是闰日。

2．英语句子的主语是由动名词、不定式词组或其他复合结构构成时，有的可以译成汉语的动宾结构、主谓结构、名词性短语或"的"字短语作句子主语。例如：

◇ Traveling to work gets more difficult and more expensive every year.
坐车去上班一年比一年难，一年比一年贵。

◇ The only way to be sure you are safe is not to drink at all.
确保安全的惟一办法就是滴酒别沾。

◇ Welcoming the New Year is one of the oldest customs celebrated the world over.
迎接新年是一种世界各地都有的最古老风俗。

◇ Driving after you've been drinking doesn't just affect you.
酒后开车不仅仅危及你本人。

3．英语句子中有主语从句、主语修饰短语或者复杂结构时，可把它译成带动宾结构、主谓结构、名词性短语或"的"字短语的汉语主语。如果不能，也可以根据情况把它译成并列分句或改用其他句子成分作主语。例如：

◇ Soya beans, which grow easily in hot climates, are now regarded as the food of the future.
在炎热气候中易于种植的大豆如今已被看做未来的食品了。

◇ For centuries the Great Wall which has fired the imagination of men surpasses all other physical human undertakings.
千百年来，激发人们想像力的长城超越了所有其他人工工程。

◇ An Englishman who saw the Great Wall in 1790 estimated that it contained more brick and stone than were to be found in the United Kingdom.
据 1790 年到过长城的一个英国人估算，长城所用的砖石数量超过了英国所能见到的。

◇ A massive campaign to persuade butchers and food-processing firms to buy the "meat" — made from soya beans — was launched by the bakery company Rank Hovis McDougall yesterday.
昨天兰克·霍维斯·麦克杜格尔面包公司展开了一场大规模宣传运动，劝说肉店和食品加工公司购买用大豆制造的"肉"。

◇ Any food containing these items must be properly marked and labeled.
任何含这类配料的食品都应该严格标明成分并贴上标签。

◇ A person's answer to the question "Is your health excellent, good, fair or poor?" is a remarkable predictor of who will live or die over the next four years.

一个人对"您的健康状况是佳、良、较好、差?"问题的回答,能对今后四年之内是否健在或死亡做出惊人的预测。

4. 有一部分英语句子的主语(例如非人指代词主语和被动句主语),按照汉语的表达习惯,翻译时需要改用其他词或词组作主语。例如:

◇ Eating anywhere in China can be such a zesty, tasty experience that words do no justice.

在中国任何地方吃饭都是一种口齿留香的体验,无法用语言来表达。

◇ Tea is drunk widely all over the world.

世界各地人们都喝茶。

◇ Being optimistic may also have its own positive effect.

乐观也可能起积极的作用。

◇ They are much cheaper than meat to produce and provide just as much protein.

这些豆制品比肉更容易生产,而且蛋白质一样多。

5. 如果英语主句和从句或并列分句中的主语相同,汉译时可以只译其中的一个,因为这类汉语复句的主语一般只出现在一个分句中。同样地,有的英语句子中的主语由于在前面的句子已经提出过,如果逻辑语气十分明确,也可以不译出来。英语被动句译成汉语时主语无法直接对译,只能改变主语或者省译主语。例如:

◇ July can be very hot, but it's always cool in the morning and evening.

七月份天气可能很热,但是早晚[　]都很凉爽。

◇ If you cycle to work you save petrol, save money and save your health.

要是你骑车去上班[　]可以节省汽油,节约钱,并有益于健康。

练　　习

1. 翻译短文:

It is said that astronauts can see the Great Wall from the moon. It is only 75 km from Beijing, and it is something the visitors can't miss. In ancient times the Chinese people built walls around their cities, and in the seventh century BC they began to build walls between rival states. Such construction continued in the Warring States Period. Later the first emperor of the Qin Dynasty had them joined together and extended as he unified the country. The section of Badaling can be reached by train or minibus. One may take a lunch box and have a picnic with friends under the shadow of the wall.

2. 翻译下列句子,注意主语的译法。

(1) He was the first ambassador to France, and he helped negotiate the treaty of 1783, which ended the civil war.

(2) The process of changing from sport car to aerocar can be done in 12 simple steps in fewer than five minutes.

(3) A passenger sitting in my compartment on the train to Beijing told me that he wanted to become a writer.

(4) It is expected that you will take care of all your own travel, living and other related personal expenses.

(5) Driving a car at night is different from driving a car during the day.

(6) To know everything is to know nothing.

(7) What may be done at any time will be done at no time.

3. 完成下列句子的翻译:

(1) Admission to some private college is more rigid than admission to some public institutions.

_____比进入一些公立院校更严格。

(2) Women working in government offices are in a minority.

_____占少数。

(3) Groups of women from "both sides of the screen" — the "professional" and the "audience" — will continue to meet to share their knowledge and ideas.

_____还将见面,共同分享知识,交换意见。

(4) Many of the problems, from the generation gap to the high divorce rate to some forms of mental illness, are caused at least in part by failure to communicate.

_____至少部分是由于缺乏交流所引起的。

(5) One of the Chinese team's three victories in France was a 16:4 win over the French national team.

_____以 16 比 4 战胜法国国家队。

(6) Visitors to provincial England sometimes find the lack of public activities in the evenings depressing.

_____有时发现晚间没有公共活动,十分沉闷。

(7) Anyone who has not attended a large college football game has missed one of the most colourful aspects of the college life.

_____没能看到校园生活多彩多姿的一面。

Lesson 24
Religions in China

The major religions in China are Taoism, Buddhism, Islam and Christianity. Of these Taoism is a native religion, the others having been introduced from foreign lands.

Taoism was founded on the teachings of Laozi, a sage born in 604 B.C. in the present-day Henan Province. He taught contemplation and retirement as a means of spiritual purification and the attainment of the *Dao*①, a principle that signifies the highest spiritual ideals of mankind. He spent his life in study and teaching. His teachings are incorporated in a profound book *Daode Jing*② which Taoists regard as the final authority and doctrines of the religion. The Taoist adherents believe that by following a certain regimen (including meditation and ascetic practices) they can attain a state bordering on immortality.③

It is generally believed that Buddhism first came to China in 67 A.D. during the reign of Emperor Mingdi of the Eastern Han Dynasty④, but the official records hold that it was first propagated in China in 2 B.C. during the reign of Emperor Aidi of the Western Han Dynasty⑤. Afterwards, because it was sanctioned by many of the successive dynasties Buddhism became widespread and had a tremendous impact on the development of Chinese thought, culture and art. Lamaism is a Buddhist sect which flourishes in the regions inhabited by the Tibetans and Mongolians. Sincere Buddhists take a vow of celibacy and abstinence from meat and wine, wear no fur or woollen garments and shave their heads.⑥

Islam first reached China about the middle of the 7th century. As commercial and cultural contacts between East and West developed, Arab and Persian traders⑦ began calling on China along the Silk Route in increasing numbers. In 651 an envoy of Moslems journeyed to Chang'an and expounded the principles of Islam to the court. There are approximately 10 million Moslems in China today, including the Huis in Ningxia and the Uighurs in Xinjiang. Nearly every major city has its mosques, shops and restaurants for Moslems.

Nestorian missionaries reached China as early as A.D. 500. Monte Corvino is regarded as the first Roman Catholic missionary to China. From the time of

Ricci to 1735 the Roman church sent five hundred missionaries all over the country. In 1807 Robert Morrison, the first British Protestant missionary to China arrived in Guangzhou. He and Milne who joined him later translated *The New Testament* into Chinese.[⑧] In 1949 Chinese Catholics totaled 3 million and Protestants 700,000.

● 注　　释 ●

① He taught contemplation and retirement as a means of spiritual purification and the attainment of the *Dao*....
他把修炼和遁世作为纯洁精神和体"道"的手段来传授……。

② *Daode Jing*
《道德经》

③ by following a certain regimen (including meditation and ascetic practices) they can attain a state bordering on immortality.
运用某种摄生法(包括入静和禁欲)可以进入长生不老的境界。

④ during the reign of Emperor Mingdi of the Eastern Han Dynasty
东汉明帝年间

⑤ during the reign of Emperor Aidi of the Western Han Dynasty
西汉哀帝年间

⑥ Sincere Buddhists take a vow of celibacy and abstinence from meat and wine, wear no fur or woollen garments and shave their heads.
虔诚的僧人立誓禁欲,不沾酒肉,不着皮毛,削发修行。

⑦ Arab and Persian traders　　　　　阿拉伯和波斯商人
the Silk Route　　　　　　　　　丝绸之路
Chang'an　　　　　　　　　　　长安
the Huis in Ningxia　　　　　　　宁夏的回族
the Uighurs in Xinjiang　　　　　新疆的维吾尔族
Nestorian missionaries　　　　　　景教传教士
Monte Corvino　　　　　　　　　孟高未诺
Roman Catholic missionary　　　　罗马天主教传教士
the time of Ricci　　　　　　　　利玛窦时代
Robert Morrison, the British Protestant missionary
英国新教传教士罗伯特·马礼逊

⑧ He and Milne who joined him later translated *The New Testament* into Chinese.
他和后来的合作者米怜共同把《新约》翻译成汉语。

※ 译法分析 ※

英语句子宾语的翻译

1. 英语及物动词谓语后的宾语(包括直接宾语和间接宾语)可以直接译为汉语的宾语,如:

◇ Isn't it out of your way if you give me a lift?
你让我搭车顺路吗?

◇ They don't like Cantonese stir-frying, but prefer steaming and simmering.
他们不喜欢广东式的炒菜,而喜欢蒸和炖。

◇ The people of the world speak different languages, but everyone understands one special language — music.
世界上人们说不同的话,但是每一个人都听得懂一种特殊的语言——音乐。

2. 有些英语动词是及物的,但是与其对应的汉语动词却可能是不及物的。相反的情况也有。英语可以说"She bathed the baby"、"He smoked himself ill",而用汉语只能说"她给孩子洗澡"、"他抽烟抽病了"。这类差异现象必然导致译文中宾语的位移,词性或句型的转换。例如:

◇ In 1969 some scientists remeasured the length of the river and found it to be 6,712 km long.
1969 年一些科学家再次对那条河进行了测量,发现其长度为 6,712 公里。

◇ A bike doesn't use expensive fuel, like petrol, but runs on manpower.
自行车不使用汽油之类的昂贵燃料,而是靠人力。

◇ The Greeks and the Romans made music by plucking strings with their fingers.
希腊人和罗马人用手指拨动琴弦弹奏乐曲。

3. 虽然英语有些动词和与其对应的汉语动词都是及物的,但是汉译时为了强调处置的过程和结果,必须用"把"字句。这样,原文中的动词宾语就变成了汉语的介词宾语了。例如:

◇ Two years ago my firm transferred me to their Paris branch.
两年前我的公司把我调到了巴黎分公司。

◇ He taught contemplation and retirement as a means of spiritual purification and the attainment of the *Dao*.
他把修炼和遁世作为纯洁精神和体"道"的手段来传授。

4. 由于汉英两种语言表达和搭配方式的差异,有一些英语句子中的宾语可以不译出来,或者改译成其他汉语句子成分。例如:

◇ The Nile used to wind *its way* through this area.

尼罗河曾经在这个地区曲折地流过。

◇ Do you still find *it* a great trouble to get up at seven o'clock in the morning?

你现在早晨7点钟起床还觉得那么无法忍受吗？

◇ You don't have large bills for repairs — a child of ten can learn to look after a bicycle.

你不必为修车付一大笔钱，一个10岁的孩子就可以学会保养自行车。

◇ I couldn't *stand playing* in the rain.

挨着雨淋打球我真受不了。

练　习

1. 翻译短文：

Poll after poll confirms these staggering figures: Nine Americans in ten say they have never doubted the existence of God; Seven in ten believe God still works miracles; Nine in ten say they pray. Among those in Western countries, Americans rank second (after Malta) in rating the importance of God in their lives. Religion does not shift or waver. So much so that more people go to churches and synagogues, in any week, than to all sports events combined. Technology, urbanization, social mobility, education—all were supposed to eat away at religion. Each has crested over America, affecting other things, but showing little power to corrode or diminish religion. In 1987, 48 percent of those polled said they would not vote for an atheist as president.

2. 翻译下列句子，注意宾语的翻译。

(1) Chinese children begin elementary school when they are six years old.

(2) Most of us spend a great part of our lives at our jobs.

(3) All they did on the farm was to plow and plant the fields, harvest the crops and milk the cows.

(4) His younger sister married a farmer and lived nearby.

(5) Almost every school child has a hobby. Some of them enjoy collecting stamps, others like making model airplanes.

(6) It is important for everyone to relax from time to time and enjoy some form of recreation after busy working or studying.

(7) Radio and television keep us informed of the daily news, instruct us in many fields of interest, and entertain us with singing and dancing.

3. 用所给的词语翻译下列句子：

(1) Those who have received a bachelor's degree will continue studying for a master's degree.　　　　　　　　　　　　　　　　　　　（已经获得学士学位的人）

(2) If it isn't too much trouble for you, could you please make these telephone calls for me?　　　　　　　　　　　　　　　　　　　（要是对你来说不太麻烦的话）

(3) I hope you won't take offence, but will accept what I may say here as some friendly advice.　　　　　　　　　　　　　　　　　　（我希望你别见怪）

(4) Most people enjoy summer weather when they can wear light weight clothes.
　　　　　　　　　　　　　　　　　　　　　　　　　（多数人都喜欢夏天的天气）

(5) She finds fault with the best movie of the year, but stays awake until 2 a.m. watching very old movies on television.
　　　　　　　　　　　　（而常常熬到凌晨两点看电视中播放的老掉牙的电影）

(6) They frequently ask the advice of their friends, but do the opposite of what their friends have suggested.　　　　　　　　　　　（他们经常征求朋友的意见）

(7) Your brothers asked me to wish you a happy birthday for them.
　　　　　　　　　　　　　　　　　　　　　　　　　　　　（祝你生日快乐）

Lesson 25
Silk

Chinese history credits sericulture to Lei Zu — the consort of the mythical Yellow Emperor[1]. Archaeologists have discovered a partially unraveled silk cocoon among the New Stone Age relics unearthed at a site in Shanxi Province.

During the Shang Dynasty[2] (c. 1600 – c. 1100 B. C.) there were already government-sponsored silk production workshops. By the time of the Zhou Dynasty (c. 1100 – 771 B.C.) the production of silk had spread as far as the Hanshui River, Huaihe River and Changjiang River valleys. The production of splendid silks with subtle designs woven into the fabric and silk decorated with coloured embroidery was soon followed by the invention of silk gauze and brocade silk. By the time of the Spring and Autumn and Warring States periods (770 – 221 B. C.), silk was manufactured throughout China. In the Tang Dynasty (618 – 907) further advances were made in weaving and dyeing techniques, resulting in even more delicate and exquisite products. Since the 17th century Zhejiang Province has become well known for its silk products.

China's geography and climate are good for the growth of mulberry and oak trees[3] of which the leaves supply natural food for two types of silkworms. The silkworms which produce fine silk have such a voracious appetite that they consume huge quantities of mulberry leaves every day. They frequently moult or cast their skins to make room for their rapid growth.[4] They then climb to the top of loose stalks of straw and begin to spin the cocoons.

The principal centres of China's sericulture industry are the plains surrounding Taihu Lake in Jiangsu Province, the Sichuan basin, the Zhujiang River delta and the Liaodong Peninsula[5].

Since ancient times, silk has been one of China's traditional exports. Fine silk products were shipped to Korea and Japan, and carried by camels running along the Silk Route and eventually reaching Western Europe.[6] Now China produces several hundred varieties of silk in thousands of colours and designs. Chinese silk products have found ready markets in more than 100 countries in the world.

① Lei Zu — the consort of the mythical Yellow Emperor

传说中的黄帝妻子嫘祖

② Shang Dynasty

商朝

Zhou Dynasty

周朝

Spring and Autumn and Warring States periods

春秋战国时期

Tang Dynasty

唐朝

the Hanshui River, Huaihe River and Changjiang River valleys

汉水、淮河和长江流域

Zhejiang Province

浙江省

③ mulberry and oak trees

桑树和柞树

④ They frequently moult or cast their skins to make room for their rapid growth.

它们经常蜕皮以便身体能够迅速增长。

⑤ Taihu Lake in Jiangsu Province, the Sichuan basin, the Zhujiang River delta and the Liaodong Peninsula

江苏省太湖、四川盆地、珠江三角洲和辽东半岛

⑥ carried by camels running along the Silk Route and eventually reaching Western Europe.

由驼队驮运,经丝绸之路最后运抵西欧。

※ 译法分析 ※

汉语使动句在英译汉中的使用

1. 现代汉语和现代英语都有很多使动句。它的特点是:谓语都含有使令意义。英语中直接表示使令意义的动词有"let"、"enable"、"make"和"cause"等。与其对等的汉语及物动词有"让"、"使"、"令"、"叫"和"促使"等。在语法上这类汉语动词可与它后面的名词和另一个动词形成兼语式结构,表明句子中前后两个动词之间存在着某种因果关系。例如:

◇ I made him run about all the time.

我始终让他跑来跑去。

◇ This makes life difficult for those who prefer to use their left hands.

这就使喜欢用左手的人的生活很不方便。

（这给喜欢用左手的人的生活带来诸多不便。）

◇ They make each day and each new acquaintance an adventure.

它使每一天以及与每一个人的结识成为新奇的经历。

2．除了上述几个常用的使动动词外，汉语和英语中都还有不少表示使动意义的其他动词。英语的一些普通动词通过词形变化可以被赋予使动意义，汉语的某些形容词作及物动词使用后也具有使动意义，这些在翻译中可以酌情使用。例如：

◇ The local supermarket saved me.

当地的超市使我免此难堪。

◇ Some supermarkets even have playrooms where mothers can leave their children while shopping.

有些超市还设立了游戏室，母亲们买东西时可以让孩子呆在那儿。

◇ At a news conference yesterday Protena was added to all kinds of delicacies and offered to journalists to taste.

在昨天的记者招待会上各种精美食品都加进了普罗特纳素肉，并让记者们品尝。

◇ To Scotsmen *Hogmanay* is a word that conjures up many pleasant associations: good whisky and first footers, to name only a few.

在苏格兰人看来，"霍格马内"这个词会使人产生许多愉快的联想，随便举个例子来说：美酒威士忌和第一批来访者。

3．英语的一些动词短语、现在分词、形容词也可以译为使动式短语。例如：

◇ satisfying　　　　　　　令人满意的

◇ exciting　　　　　　　　令人兴奋的

◇ to one's surprise　　　　令人奇怪的

============练　　习============

1．翻译短文：

The land around Hangzhou is fertile and good for the production of its silk and tea. The extensive tracts of mulberry trees there supply the local filatures. Hangzhou's silk industry established in the 7th century, is famous throughout China. A popular saying recommends that one should be born in Suzhou because the women are beautiful, and should be clothed in Hangzhou for its fine silk. There are silk dyeing and printing mills where workers engage in the various stages of production from reeling silk fibre off the silkworm cocoons to printing designs on the finished fabric. Silk products are made here both for export throughout the world and for domestic consumption.

2. 翻译下列句子:

(1) His ideas were too strange to please the men who hired him, so they told him to leave.

(2) To most people it is difficult to explain why the scientist's theory eventually shook the whole intellectual world.

(3) She was amazed to hear that the prices were so much higher there than they used to be.

(4) Your parcel was a great surprise as I had not expected anyone to remember my birthday.

(5) My train to Shanghai is about to leave soon, which makes time too short for me to write more about my journey in this letter.

(6) A careless man, he caused trouble to all of his friends.

(7) His great scientific inventions made him universally respected.

3. 从右边的汉语短句中选择恰当的翻译,将所代表的字母填入相关的括号内。

(　)Please don't disappoint her.	A. 别叫她难堪。
(　)He asked an amazing question.	B. 他问了一个令人迷惑不解的问题。
(　)They were shocked at the news.	C. 这消息使他们吃了一惊。
(　)The news astonished them.	D. 这报道使他们惊讶不已。
(　)Her behaviour was disgusting.	E. 别让她失望。
(　)The news gave them a start.	F. 这新闻使他们大为震惊。
(　)What startling news!	G. 多么使人激动的消息!
(　)Don't put her in an awkward situation.	H. 她的行为令人恶心。
(　)What exciting news!	I. 多么令人吃惊的消息!
(　)Don't distress yourself.	J. 真叫人讨厌!
(　)He asked a puzzling question.	K. 他问了一个令人吃惊的问题。
(　)What's worrying you?	L. 别使自己烦恼。
(　)How annoying!	M. 什么事使你烦恼?

Lesson 26
Roman Descendants

In May 1993 some Chinese and foreign archaeologists discovered that the Lijian Ruins were actually a very old town built in the Western Han Dynasty (206 BC – AD 23), in Zhelaizhai Village, Gansu Province.① There they excavated dozens of iron cauldrons, pots, ceramic kettles and big logs used by soldiers.② All the relics were verified as the evidence of a Roman connection with the village. Had any Romans come to Gansu? But China had never fought a war with Rome due to the distance between the two countries.

Historians have found the key to the question that had remained unsolved for nearly 2,000 years. In 53 BC seven legions of Roman soldiers invaded Parthia, present-day Iran. Having been defeated they wandered into China and settled at the foot of the Qilianshan Mountains.③ Two Chinese generals and their men encountered them drilling with their round shields in a barrack surrounded by huge logs. 1,500 Romans were captured and brought to Lijian, a county named after their original country (the Roman Republic was known as *Lijian* in ancient China).

Archaeologists found that many villagers in Lijian have high-bridged noses, deep-set eyes, curly blond hair and large-boned figures like Europeans.④ There are some unique customs in the area. The local people often make ox-head shaped bread from leavened flour as a sacrificial offering.⑤ They built Ox God Temple in the village shrines and at major crossroads, and erected ox heads as symbols. Ox Butting is a favorite sport there. It is believed that the custom has something to do with the bullfighting popular with the ancient Romans.⑥

● 注　　释 ●

① the Lijian Ruins were actually an old town built in the Western Han Dynasty (206 BC – AD23), in Zhelaizhai Village, Gansu Province.
甘肃省蔗贲寨的骊轩遗址实际上是西汉(公元前 206 年~公元 23 年)所建的一座古城。

② excavated dozens of iron cauldrons, pots, ceramic kettles and big logs used by soldiers.

发掘出几十件士兵使用的铁锅、水罐、瓷壶和巨木。

③ seven legions of Roman soldiers invaded Parthia, present-day Iran. Having been defeated they wandered into China and settled at the foot of the Qilianshan Mountains.

7 个罗马军团入侵安息(今伊朗),被击败后来到中国,扎营于祁连山下。

④ have high-bridged noses, deep-set eyes, curly blond hair and large-boned figures like Europeans.

像欧洲人那样,高鼻梁,凹眼睛,卷曲黄头发,身材高大。

⑤ often make ox-head shaped bread from leavened flour as a sacrificial offering.

常用发面做成牛头形馒头作供品。

⑥ the custom has something to do with the bullfighting popular with the ancient Romans.

这一风俗可能与古代罗马人喜欢斗牛有关。

※ 译法分析 ※

汉语"把"字句在英译汉中的使用

1. "把"字句是汉语中常用的一种特殊句式。它通过介词"把"和一个名词组成介宾短语作句子中谓语的状语,表示一种处置或使动意义。"把"字句的表达作用是其他句式所不能代替的,英语中没有相似的结构。

◇ These picnic suppers were usually held indoors in well decorated dining rooms, but sometimes tables were laid outside in the gardens of stately homes.

这种自带食品的晚餐通常在装饰漂亮的餐厅里举行,但有时也把餐桌摆到豪门大宅的花园里。

◇ It takes about an hour for the body to get rid of the alcohol in one standard drink.

大概需要一个小时人体才能把一次标准饮量中的酒精消除。

◇ Historians have found the key to the question that had remained unsolved for nearly 2,000 years.

历史学家把近 2000 年一直没有解决的疑团揭开了。

2. 什么样的英文句子可以用"把"字句来翻译? A. 表示处置意思的句子; B. 部分表示使动意思的句子;C. 带双宾语的句子(包括"介词 + 间接宾语"短语的句子);D. 带其他及物动词谓语的句子。请看下面的例句:

◇ Those who rate their health "poor" are four to five times more likely to die in the next four years than those who rate their health "excellent".

那些把自己的健康情况列为"差"的人在今后四年之内死亡的可能性，比那些把自己的健康情况列为"佳"的人高 4~5 倍。

◇ But link a human brain with a machine, and what of the individual then?

但是若把人脑跟一台机器连接起来,那还有什么个人可言?

◇ The "beggars' chicken" is prepared by covering it with special clay and stuffing it with lotus seeds.

"叫花子鸡"的做法是把莲子放入鸡膛内,外面用一种特别的泥包裹着。

◇ The sights of Beijing are so numerous that one can spend several weeks here and leave without having seen all of the important ones.

北京的名胜很多,一个人就是在这儿呆上几个星期,离开时也不会把主要的景点看完。

◇ In the third century B.C. the great Emperor Shi Huangdi of the Qin Dynasty ordered the separate sections of the walls linked together to form the basis of the present Great Wall.

公元前 3 世纪时秦始皇下令把各段城墙连接起来,这便是现在长城的基础。

━━━━━━ 练　　习 ━━━━━━

1. 翻译短文:

China is a multinational country comprising 56 major ethnic groups or nationalities. Tibetans live in Tibet, Qinghai and part of Sichuan. The Moslems including the Uighurs, Kazakhs and Kirghiz live in Xinjiang, Gansu and Qinghai. The Mongolians live in the area along the border with the People's Republic of Mongolia. The Manchus and Koreans live in the northeast. Living in the uplands in southwest China are the Dais, Zhuangs and Buyis. The Miaos and Yaos live in southern Guizhou and Yunnan. The Zhuangs number some 8 million; the smallest group is the Hezhes of whom the population is over 1000.

2. 用"把"字句翻译下列句子:

(1) The postman delivers the newspaper to your door every day.

(2) Please take the luggage upstairs.

(3) He removed the paper that the big box was wrapped in.

(4) He took his blue coat to the dry cleaner's and left his shirts at the laundry.

(5) Every day my husband puts the garbage in the backyard before going to work.

(6) It's hard for the children to remember the names of all their relatives who don't often come for a visit.

(7) The boy sleeps so well that even a military band nearby cannot wake him up.

3. 用"把"字短语完成下列句子的翻译：

(1) Will it be possible for you to explain your plans to him?

_____说一说，可以吗？

(2) Please let me know what you have decided.

_____告诉我。

(3) She put all the heavy things in the suitcase, and added the lighter ones to it.

她先_____，然后_____。

(4) He was unable to drive his car into his garage.

_____开到车库里去。

(5) My next-door neighbour sometimes parks his car in front of my house.

我的隔壁邻居有时_____。

(6) They had to cut down many trees to make room for their farms.

为了给农场腾地方他们_____。

Lesson 27
Error Analysis

实例一

英文原文

① It's been raining for several days with no end in sight. ② I've been spending the day sitting at my desk from morning till night. ③ My desk stands in front of the window, and when I look up I can see raindrops dripping down the surface of the glass. ④ All I can hear is the monotonous patter of raindrops on the flagstones beneath the window. ⑤This sound has continued without variation for the last few days. ⑥ At first I barely noticed anything, but gradually I became more aware of it. ⑦ Before long it became such a torment that I could hardly concentrate on my reading. ⑧ Finally I was no longer able to make out the words on the page.

学生译文

①下雨了,已经好几天了,而看样子还要下。② 我从上午一直到晚上都在我写字台坐着。③ 桌子是在窗口前面,而我每一次往上看就见到玻璃上滴滴答答的雨点。④ 惟一可听到是那窗口外面板石上下雨的答答声音单调。⑤ 这声音近日一直不变了。⑥ 刚开始我不太注意这个,但过了一阵儿我越来越注意。⑦ 不久是那样的折腾我,就什么书也看不进去了。⑧ 最后我是看一页,字也都看不清了。

错误分析

① 第一句译文有三处不妥:一、原文句子较短,把它拆译成三个更短的短语显得太零碎了;二、汉语"下雨了"中的"了",一般用来表示情况有所变化,译文与原意不符;三、"而"字所连接的两部分既不相互承接又无相反的意思。全句可译为"雨已经下了好几天了,看样子还没有停的意思"。

② 第二句"my desk"中的"my"按照汉语表达习惯可以不译出来。"在我写字台坐着"可能被错误理解为"坐在写字台上"。全句可译为"我从早到晚一直坐在写字台旁",或"终日伏案"。

94

③ 第三句译文中的"窗口面前"欠妥。汉语"窗口"有两个意思，一是指"窗户跟前"，二是指"买票或挂号的窗形开口"，原文指第一个意思。"桌子"与第二句的"写字台"都是"desk"的翻译，似乎指两件家具。后半句译文意思不确切。全句可改译为"写字台摆在窗前，我一仰头就看得见雨点顺着玻璃往下滴"。

④ 第四句译文"惟一可听到的是……声音单调"，搭配不当，意思也不确切。可改译为"我听到的只是雨点打在窗下石板上单调的滴答声"。

⑤ 第五句译文中的"了"用得不恰当，因为原文不是指"情况有变化"。可改译为"这几天来这声音持续不变"。

⑥ 第六句译文基本通顺，但不够确切，可改译为"刚开始我几乎什么都没觉察，但慢慢地才引起了注意"。

⑦ 第七句译文前半句没有主语，欠通顺。"torment"应为"折磨"而不是"折腾"。可改译为"很快这竟成了一种折磨人的声音，于是我再也无法专心致志地看书了"。

⑧ 第八句译文也有语病，意思不清楚。英语的"word"是"词"而不是"字"。可改译为"后来我连书上那些话的意思都弄不明白了"。

实例二

英文原文

① Rice was, and still is, one of the most widely eaten foods in China. ② It is grown along the valley of the Yangtse River and in South China where the climate is warm and wet enough. ③ The people in the Northern cities got their rice from the south, it came up the Grand Canal in barges. ④ Rice is so important as a food that the word for cooked rice means a meal; to invite someone to a meal you ask him to come to eat rice. ⑤ Generally rice is served in individual bowls, and vegetables, meat and fish are served in communal dishes from which everyone helps himself. ⑥ It is all eaten with chopsticks and therefore has to be cut up very small.

学生译文

① 中国今昔最普遍的饭是大米。② 长江流域及气候湿热的南方地区都是米粮川。③ 北方人过去用驳船而通过大运河进口了华南的米。④ 大米作为食品是那么重要，在中文里头就把做熟的大米这个字等于餐的意思。当你请人到你家来吃饭，实际上你在请他来吃米饭。⑤ 米饭平常是一个人一个碗上的，而菜、肉和鱼是在大碗里摆在桌子上，然后大家随便吃。⑥ 因为用筷子吃，他们做饭时把菜切成小块儿。

① 第一句译文中的"……饭是大米"逻辑欠通顺。"今昔"是名词,用作"饭"的定语意思和语体都不协调。全句应译为"在中国,大米过去是现在仍然是人们最普遍吃的一种粮食"。

② 第二句译文中的"米粮川"多用于比喻盛产粮食的大片良田。"川"指山间或高原间的平坦地带。就整体而言,用"米粮川"来描述长江流域和南方不很得体。这句话可改译为"它生长在长江流域沿岸和气候湿热的南方"。

③ 第三句译文中的"而"用法欠妥。另外,汉语"进口"多用于指从外国输入货物。全句可改译为"过去北方的市民都用驳船通过大运河从南方运进大米"。

④ 第四句译文中"把……等于餐的意思"语法不通。"做熟的大米"应为"米饭"。全句可改译为"大米是一种主要的粮食,因此'饭'这个词就是'一顿饭'的意思;'宴请某人'就是'请某人吃饭'"。

⑤ 第五句译文"一个人一个碗上的"不通,"随便吃"也不确切。全句可改译为"通常米饭都盛到个人的碗里,而蔬菜、肉和鱼之类都盛在公盘里,每个人可以自己夹。"

⑥ 第六句译文基本通顺,但是"他们做饭时"多余。全句可改译为"因为用筷子吃,所以菜得切成小块儿"。

小结

1．对于英语国家的留学生来说,学习英汉翻译课的主要困难是汉语表达中的语法、词汇和文化背景的理解问题。对于非英语国家的留学生来说,如果英语水平不高,就可能会同时碰到对于原文意思的准确理解和汉语表达的问题。学生应该根据自己的条件克服困难,明确自己的难点和努力方向。

2．一般来说,把有一定难度的英文翻译成汉语时,可以直译的句子数量极少。如果自己的译文跟原文对照起来,有许多句子结构、语序、表达方式相同的话,就应该对自己的译文是否符合汉语习惯加以思考,必要时应该反复推敲和检查。

3．外国留学生在翻译中可能碰到的汉语表达问题主要有:对于多义项词语的理解和选择问题;对于词语的使用域的确定问题;对于词语的文化内涵的理解问题,等等。

4．学生应该养成对于所做作业进行检查和修改的良好习惯和认真作风。自己没有把握的问题应该查辞典或向他人请教。

把下列短文翻译成汉语：

(1) One day my father was working outdoors. A car pulled up in front of our house and a woman came out of it, hailing him for directions to go to the the down town.

"Follow this road to the end and go right," he said. "Turn left two times and right two times. It's a quarter-mile on the right."

She thanked him and drove away. About 20 minutes later the same woman pulled up again, calling, "Mister...." My father looked up in time to see her eyes widen in recognition. "Never mind," she said, and zoomed off.

(2) A group of researchers tested the physical fitness of more than 13,000 healthy men and women, and followed them for an average of eight years. Their fitness was measured by performance on a treadmill, rather than by relying on verbal reports of exercise. The researchers discovered that even modest amounts of exercise can substantially reduce a person's chances of dying of heart disease, cancer or other causes; that going from being sedentary to walking briskly for a half hour several days a week can drop a person's risk dramatically.

(3) Don't go looking for spring just down the road. All you will find is March. The vernal equinox now is just weeks ahead, true; but spring isn't a date on a calendar, and it isn't astronomical calculation set down in an almanac. Spring is a new sprout, an unfolding leaf, a blossom and a bee. It is brooks chattering across the meadows and peepers shrilling in the boglands in the dusk.

Lesson 28
Leaving Home

After 35 years we had to move out of our home. How does one say good-bye to a house? As the stalwart moving men maneuvered our bedroom furniture into their van, I thought back to the nights when thunder and lightning drove our two small daughters from their rooms and under our covers.① Those same two girls, now grown women, came by to say a fond farewell to "their house." They walked from room to room, laughing and crying, recalling events that shaped their lives. Walls echoed with the same sounds of yesterday; finger-smudged doors slammed in my memory.②

Three and a half decades before, we had come to this house with joy and anticipation. We watched our house grow and take on a majesty no castle could equal. Warmth and caring wallpapered our rooms. We celebrated every event.③ Not all the years were joyous. Sickness and loss of dear ones plagued us constantly. But, always, the comforting embrace of our house welcomed us and helped renew our spirits. We grew old, but not so our house. Guarded by tall trees and flowering bushes,④ it became more beautiful, more confident, more solid.

The new caretakers of our house were young. We prayed they would be happy. We knew we would never live in our house again. But memories are sustaining, and we have no regrets.⑤

(By Charlotte Rosenstock)

● 注　释 ●

① I thought back to the nights when thunder and lightning drove our two small daughters from their rooms and under our covers.
不禁使我回想起那些电闪雷鸣之夜吓得两个小女儿从房间跑出钻进我们的被窝里的情形。

② Walls echoed with the same sounds of yesterday; finger-smudged doors slammed in my memory.
四壁回荡着与往日一样的响声,留着指痕的房门在我的记忆中已嘭然关上。

98

③ Warmth and caring wallpapered our rooms. We celebrated every event.

温馨和关爱笼罩着居室,我们为每一件事而庆幸。

④ Guarded by tall trees and flowering bushes....

有大树绿荫笼罩和吐蕊灌木相衬……。

⑤ But memories are sustaining, and we have no regrets.

然而记忆却是永不休止的,我们觉得无怨无悔!

※ 译法分析 ※

汉语词语搭配理论在英译汉中的使用

1. 汉语的"词语搭配",主要是指句子中的主语与谓语、主语与宾语、谓语与宾语、定语、状语、补语与中心语之间,在意义上、语法上、风格上、逻辑上和语用习惯上是否协调通顺,是否符合约定俗成的规则。英语中的固定词组也属于词语搭配现象,例如"too...to"、"keep from doing"、"can do with"、"do away with"、"do well"、"do up"等,改变其中一个词,也许不符合语法,也许意义不相同。又如,用英语可以说"make tea"(沏茶)、"brew tea"(泡茶),但是不能说"soak tea";可以说"eat out"(吃馆子),但是不能说"eat a restaurant",可以说"prepare a meal"(做饭),但是不能说"make a meal"。不过,汉语的搭配范围、方式和要求比英语更为严格些。翻译时不注意搭配问题,译文的质量就可能不高。试比较:

◇ Is that enough off the top?

离开顶上那么多够不够?

(顶上的头发去掉那么多够吗?)

◇ The Greeks and Romans made music by plucking strings with their fingers.

希腊人和罗马人用手指拨弦制造音乐。

(希腊人和罗马人用手指拨动琴弦弹奏乐曲。)

◇ the nights when thunder and lightning drove our two daughters from their rooms

晚上雷和电把我们的两个女儿驱赶出她们的房间

(在那雷鸣电闪之夜我们的两个小女儿被吓得从房间跑了出来)

◇ those same two girls, now grown women

同样两个姑娘,现在的成年妇女

(当年两个小丫头如今已出落成少妇)

◇ And it was cheap, I discovered. I was converted.

和很便宜,我发现。我被改变信仰。

(而且我还发现东西很便宜,这使我折服。)

2. 把英语短语或句子翻译成汉语时应该按照汉语的词语搭配方式,如果直译过来就可能不通顺,甚至改变了原意,或者译文无法被读者接受。例如:

◇ farmmer do their ploughing

农民做耕种

（农民耕种）

◇ I might well have a shampoo while I'm at it.

我在的时候可能要一个香波。

（我顺便洗个头吧。）

◇ All the relics were verified as the evidence of a Roman connection with the village.

所有的遗物被证明是罗马与这个村子联系的证据。

（这些文物证实了罗马人与这个寨子的某种关系。）

◇ We watched our house grow and take on a majesty no castle equal.

我们看见我们的房子长大和呈现庄严面貌，没有碉堡等同。

（我们看着这个家在扩大，变得堂皇起来，无与伦比。）

◇ guarded by tall trees and flowering bushes

被高大的树和开花的灌木保护着

（有大树绿阴笼罩和吐蕊灌木相衬）

3．一个多义项的英文单词，在翻译中应该根据它在实际使用中的含义来选择相应的汉语词语。两者的意义越贴切，风格和语用越接近，译文的质量就可能越高。千万不能照搬字典，否则就会出现误译或死译的情况。例如：

◇ traveling musicians

旅游音乐家

（江湖艺人）

◇ save your health

节省你的健康

（保持健康）

◇ in the open air

在开放空气中

（在露天）

◇ reproductive bank

生殖银行

（繁殖库）

◇ moving men

活动人

（搬家工人）

◇ They walked from room to room.

她们从一个房间散步到另一个房间。

（她们从一个房间走到另一个房间。）

◇ helped renew our spirits

帮助更新我们的精神

（使我们得以进入更新的精神境界）

═══════ 练　　习 ═══════

1. 翻译短文：

I shall long cherish the memory of that delightful evening I spent at home. My wife and I had a simple dinner alone, with pleasant and interesting conversation. Then we sat at the piano and sang many of our favourite songs. When our throats grew weary, we turned on the stereo and danced to beautiful music. When our breath became short, we strolled, arm-in-arm, through our moonlit yard. I was so very happy, and I longed for more such evenings. But, alas—early the next morning, a truck pulled into our driveway and shattered my hope. It was the TV repairman.

2. 翻译下列句子：

(1) a globe of the world

(2) open your eyes

(3) the medium size suitcase

(4) get plenty of exercise

(5) perform a successful operation

(6) an ear, nose and throat specialist

(7) take a good rest

(8) enjoy seeing some photos of you

(9) behave very strangely

3. 完成以下多项选择，在正确意思前画圈。

(1) We've already rented the house to somebody else.

　　A. 我们早就租房子给别人了。

　　B. 我们已把房子租给了别人。

　　C. 咱们已经对另外的人出租了房屋。

　　D. 咱们已经出租了房子给另外的人。

(2) I guess I've outgrown this pair of trousers.

    A．我猜测我已经生长速度超过这条裤子了。

    B．我想我已经比这裤子长大了。

    C．我估计这裤子比我长大了。

    D．我想自己已经长高,这条裤子穿不了了。

(3) I don't see any point in discussing the question any further.

    A．我看不见进一步讨论这个问题中的点。

    B．我不明白再讨论这个问题有什么意义。

    C．我不能看继续讨论这个问题的意义。

    D．我不清楚还谈这个问题的任何要点。

(4) There's a chance he won't be able to be home for the New Year.

    A．可能他赶不回家去过年了。

    B．有机会他不能回家过年了。

    C．可能他将不能为过年而回家。

    D．他不能回家过年的机会是有的。

(5) She couldn't stand him, and he couldn't stand her.

    A．她不让他站,并且他不让她站。

    B．她不能站住他,他也不能站住她。

    C．他们都互相不允许对方站住。

    D．她容忍不了他,他也容忍不了她。

Lesson 29
The Secret World of Pandas

It is such an odd relationship, this affair between people and pandas. We are so adoring of them that when the Chinese Government lent a pair to the San Diego Zoo[①] for six months, attendance soared[②], and the zoo sold over half a million panda T-shirts. When a panda was born in a Tokyo zoo in 1986, thousands of people phoned daily to hear a recording of the baby's cry.

Although the reason we love pandas is not easy to explain, animal behaviorists offer some plausible theories. Parenting instincts are aroused, as ethologist Konrad Lorenz[③] suggested, by the common characteristics of babies — round faces, wobbly gaits and small jaws. Pandas, even in roly-poly adulthood[④], display all of these appealing features.

Until recently, however, it seemed nearly certain that this much-loved creature was destined to die out. The panda's habitat is fast disappearing. Scientists estimate that panda communities of fewer than 100 animals face serious inbreeding problems[⑤]; of all the panda communities in China, only a few have populations of 50 or more. Logging, mining and road-building impinge on the remaining bamboo highlands, the panda's main source of food. A peculiar characteristic of bamboo is that whole communities of the plant flower simultaneously and then promptly die. These massive flowerings and die-offs occur at unpredictable intervals, and the time between them can be as long as 100 years.[⑥] When the panda's bamboo territory becomes unnaturally small, the death of the plants can spell starvation.

But an untimely end for the world's most beloved wild species may still be avoidable. "It's easy to save the panda," says George Schaller, the New York Zoological Society's panda expert and a world renowned zoologist [⑦]. "All it needs is bamboo and peace."

Wildlife experts have recommended some basic steps to help. A detailed plan for protection of the panda has been drawn up by the World Wildlife Fund, in cooperation with the Chinese Ministry of Forestry. The plan calls for a 70-percent increase in the panda preserves at a cost of about $ 20 million over five years.[⑧] The Chinese people have established 13 panda reserves and announced plans for 14 more. Public concern for the welfare of pandas has been heightened. These captivating creatures clearly hold a special place in our hearts.⑨

(An abridged text from *Boston Globe Magazine*)

● 注　释 ●

① the San Diego Zoo
圣迭各动物园

② attendance soared
参观人数激增

③ ethologist Konrad Lorenz
个体生态学家康拉德·洛伦茨

④ even in roly-poly adulthood
即便在体态敦实的成年阶段

⑤ panda communities of fewer than 100 animals face serious inbreeding problems
总数不足 100 只的熊猫群体都面临着近亲繁殖的严重问题

⑥ These massive flowerings and die-offs occur at unpredictable intervals, and the time between them can be as long as 100 years.
这种大面积开花和死亡的间隔周期无法预测,时间可长达 100 年。

⑦ George Schaller, the New York Zoological Society's panda expert and a world renowned zoologist
纽约动物学会熊猫专家、世界著名动物学家乔治·沙勒

⑧ The plan calls for a 70-percent increase in the panda preserves at a cost of about $ 20 million over five years.
计划要求 5 年中耗资 2000 万美元增加 70%的熊猫保护区。

⑨ These captivating creatures clearly hold a special place in our hearts.
显然,这些有魅力的生灵在我们心中占有一个特殊的地位。

※ 译法分析 ※

拆译与合译

英译汉时常会碰到一些比较复杂的长句和比较简单的短句,如果按照原文翻译,有的长句显得累赘臃肿,而有的短句则显得琐屑零碎。假如这些句式过多地出现在一篇文章中,就会使译文在风格上紊乱失调。所谓"长"和"短",是根据两种语言的语法和修辞规则以及原文文体的风格来决定的。

为了使译文通顺流畅,可以用拆译(长句短译)和合译(短句合译)的方法解决上述问题。拆译和合译主要是扩展或紧缩原文句子结构,在不损失不添加意思的前提下,用另一种语言方式再现原文的精神实质。

拆译的句子不一定都是长句。如果某一个词或句子的组成部分可以并且必须独立出来,就可以另译成句。拆译的具体做法有:1. 把原文句子中的单词译成词组或者单句;2. 把词组译成单句或者复句;3. 把一个单句译成两个以上的单句或者一个复句;4. 把一个复句译成两个以上的复句、多重复句或者其他更复杂的句式。例如:

◇ The Great Wall remains today as it has been for more than twenty centuries the only work of men that is visible from the moon.

长城至今已存在 2000 多年,是从月球上可以看到的惟一人工建筑。

◇ The construction of the wall began in the seventh century B.C. when separate feudal states in northern China built barriers against invasions by neighbouring states along their borders.

长城始建于公元前 7 世纪。当时北方的诸侯为了阻挡周边国家的入侵各自建筑了自己的城墙。

◇ He taught contemplation and retirement as a means of spiritual purification and the attainment of the *dao*, a principle that signifies the highest spiritual ideals of mankind.

他把修炼和遁世作为纯洁精神和体"道"的手段来传授。"道"是人类最高的精神理想。

◇ We are so adoring of them that when the Chinese Government lent a pair to the San Diego Zoo for six months, attendance soared, and the zoo sold over half a million panda T-shirts.

我们喜欢熊猫已经到了无以复加的程度,因此当中国政府借给圣迭各动物园一对熊猫半年时,参观者人数激增,该动物园售出印有熊猫图案的 T 恤衫竟达 50 万件之多。

合译的具体做法有:1. 把原文句子中的一个或几个词组译成一个单词;2. 把单句译成词组;3. 把两个以上的单句译成一个单句或一个复句;4. 把一个复句或多重复句译为一个单句;5. 把几个复句、多重复句或其他更复杂的句式译为一个复句。例如:

◇ The wall traverses plains and mountains being at some points 1300 metres above sea level. The wall averaged 7.8 metres in height and 5.8 metres at the top.

长城跨越平原高山,在某些地方海拔 1300 米,平均高 7.8 米,顶宽 5.8 米。

◇ The last day of the year, known in England as New Year's Eve, has a different name in Scotland. There it is called *Hogmanay*.

一年的最后一天在英格兰被称为除夕,而在苏格兰却另有一个名字,叫做"霍格马内"。

◇ In 53 B.C. seven legions of Roman soldiers invaded Parthis, present-day Iran. Having been defeated they wandered into China and settled at the foot of the Qilianshan Mountains.

公元前53年7个罗马军团入侵安息(今伊朗),被击败后来到中国,扎营于祁连山下。

◇ It is such an odd relationship, this affair between people and pandas.

人与熊猫的关系有点异乎寻常。

═══════════ 练　习 ═══════════

1. 翻译短文:

Dolphins have become a popular attraction at zoos in recent years. They are more interesting than lions and tigers because they are livelier and perform tricks, like circus animals. But although they are more willing to cooperate with the trainer than other mammals in captivity, they get bored if they are asked to do the same trick twice. This is one reason for believing that they are very intelligent. They are regarded as the friendliest creatures in the sea and stories of them helping drowning sailors have been common since Roman times.

2. 完成下列句子的翻译:

(1) She gave him an argument for causing her so much inconvenience.

　　她跟他争论了一番,＿＿＿＿＿＿＿＿＿＿＿＿＿＿＿＿＿＿＿。

(2) Nutrition experts have studied foods and what they do for the human body.

　　营养专家对食品进行了研究,＿＿＿＿＿＿＿＿＿＿＿＿＿＿＿＿＿。

(3) He was so successful that he was able to open his own school when he was only twenty-five.

　　他的事业很成功,＿＿＿＿＿＿＿＿＿＿＿＿＿＿＿＿＿＿＿。

(4) Peter took a long walk in the rain without a raincoat or an umbrella.

　　彼得在雨中走了很久,＿＿＿＿＿＿＿＿＿＿＿＿＿＿＿＿＿。

(5) Sign language is everybody's second language that is in use in all parts of the world.

　　手势语是每一个人的第二语言,＿＿＿＿＿＿＿＿＿＿＿＿＿＿＿＿。

(6) Carefully Audrey Peterson raised the window shade enough to let the sunlight

106

steam into her bedroom.

奥德丽·彼得森把窗帘_____。

(7) She turned down the television and a moment later we heard someone calling for help.

她把电视的声音调小,_____。

3. 用拆译法和合译法翻译下列句子:

(1) With about 8,250 undergraduates like John Smith and over 2,000 postgraduates, Cambridge is a busy place in term time.

(2) He was a well-known teacher. He developed a system called "Visible Speech" which he used to teach deaf people to speak.

(3) Our bodies need good materials to build and repair bones, teeth and muscles. They need fuel for energy. And they need material that will control the way the body works.

(4) Mr. White, an old friend of grandfather's, visited us from time to time. The old man could not talk well. He stuttered.

(5) I banged on the door but the old lady took a long time to answer. I was turning over in my mind the idea of breaking the door down when she finally appeared.

(6) We may as well go in and see the film. It would be a pity to miss it after all this waiting.

(7) I have just seen your advertisement in *The Sunday Times* of 12th April for a guide to accompany parties of British tourists in southern China during the summer months.

Lesson 30
Understanding China

Having been in China for several years now, I am often approached by new comers for advice on how to understand the thinking of our Chinese friends, colleagues and neighbours. If there's one thing I've learned, it's that every answer I hit on only leads to more questions.①

Some of the lessons I have learned about how Chinese people think and act have been of real value in dealing with friends and colleagues, as well as in handling casual contacts on the street or in shops.② Over and over I observe that in certain common situations Chinese and Westerners behave quite differently.

For instance, if Westerners find themselves in an embarrassing situation, they usually offer an explanation as a way to extricate themselves from their embarrassment. But the average Chinese person will begin to laugh. For a Westerner, this takes some getting used to. When you confront someone with an issue and that person starts to giggle in your face, it can readily lead to unpleasant misinterpretations of his attitude.③ But understanding that the laughter is itself a sign of embarrassment, not an indication that the other person fails to understand the seriousness of the problem, helps me to take the Chinese reaction in stride and move on to a solution.

Here's another example of a contrast in behaviour. Most Americans don't try to settle arguments by shouting, which usually signals an escalation of the conflict, not an impending solution. Here in China, I've had people raise their voices to me and assume very menacing postures over the tiniest of issues.④ At these times I have to bear in mind that this is probably not an invitation to a boxing match. In fact, arguments rarely turn violent in China, although I've heard plenty of yelling and abusive language. It's hard for Americans to understand what all the shouting is about when the people involved are not actually angry enough to fight over the issue. For Americans, if the matter is a small one, it's too much of an effort to get all worked up over it.⑤

Another cultural difference that stands out has to do with trying not to offend people — but failing miserably in the process. When I was still living in the States, I was amazed by the inability of my Chinese friends to say "no". This

108

could often be awkward. For example, I might ask a friend of mine to eat dinner at my place on a Saturday evening. Not wishing to give offense, the friend would accept the invitation. But then, when Saturday night came and went without a sign of the friend for dinner, I would indeed be offended. Apparently the friend just couldn't bring himself to say "no" even if he had other plans he couldn't break.⑥

I was amazed to discover that "no" is a very common word in the Chinese vocabulary, and much used in government offices. Saying "no" is a sure way not to make a mistake: "No, you can't do that." "No, that's not possible." Somehow "no" is the easiest answer to give when facing a difficult decision.

Although I constantly note differences between myself and my Chinese friends, I'm never discouraged. On the contrary, it is these differences that are the spice of life for me in China. They make each day and each new acquaintance an adventure.

(By Richard Pierce)

● 注　　释 ●

① If there's one thing I've learned, it's that every answer I hit on only leads to more questions.
如果说我学到了一点什么,那就是我偶尔得到的每一个答案又引出了更多的问题。

② have been of real value in dealing with friends and colleagues, as well as in handling casual contacts on the street or in shops.
对于跟朋友和同事打交道以及在街头或商店与人的随便接触都是非常有价值的。

③ and that person starts to giggle in your face, it can readily lead to unpleasant misinterpretations of his attitude.
那个人冲你吃吃地笑起来,这很容易使你对他的态度做出不愉快的解释。

④ I've had people raise their voices to me and assume very menacing postures over the tiniest of issues.
我碰到过一些人为鸡毛蒜皮的事抬高嗓门冲我嚷,并摆出一副威胁人的架势。

⑤ if the matter is a small one, it's too much of an effort to get all worked up over it.
如果那是一件区区小事,为它激动上火那就未免小题大做了。

⑥ Apparently the friend just couldn't bring himself to say "no" even if he had other plans he couldn't break.

显然,即便这位朋友还有其他无法失约的事要做他也不能让自己说出一个"不"字来。

※ 译法分析 ※

词类转换法

"词类"是指词汇在语法上的分类,例如:"名词"、"动词"、"形容词"、"副词"、"数词"、"量词"、"介词"等。由于表达方式的差异,按照原文中的词类直译过来的句子往往是不通顺的。为了使译文易读易懂,更准确地表达原文的意义和风格,翻译时常常要根据语法需要使用与原文词类不同的词语。这样,在多数情况下译文句子结构的成分与原文的结构成分有所不同,因此每个词与原文中对应的词类也不完全一样。

一般来说,汉语句子中的动词数量多于对应的英语句子中的动词,而英语句子中的名词则往往多于相应的汉语句子中的名词,所以把名词转译为动词是英译汉时经常进行的一项词类转换。英语句子中的名词、介词、形容词和副词都可能转译成动词。此外,英语的动词、形容词、副词可以转换成汉语的名词,有些名词和动词可以转换成副词,名词、介词、动词可以转换成汉语的形容词。这样的转换可以根据实际情况进行,没有什么限制。例如:

◇ It also meant the end of the Saturday street market in the area.
这也意味着该地区星期六街头集市就此结束。 (名词→动词)

◇ Did you know that there have been only 14 people that have lived for more than 110 years?
你是否知道只有 14 个人的寿命超过了 110 岁? (动词→名词)

◇ They claim that their product, Protena, tastes, smells and looks just like meat.
他们声称他们的产品普罗特纳色、香、味都和肉一样。 (动词→名词)

◇ You will see that some of the monkeys prefer to swing from their right hands and others will use their left hands.
你会看到有些猴子喜欢用右前肢荡秋千,而另外一些则用左前肢荡秋千。 (介词→动词)

◇ Children often go to school by bike and students cycle to class.
孩子们经常骑自行车去上学,学生们骑自行车去上课。 (介词→动词)

◇ It is very difficult to be sure of the age of very old people.
老年人的年龄很难确定。 (形容词→动词)

◇ As for the North Pole — we know that it is not only a <u>dangerously cold</u> place, but that people like you and me would find it quite impossible to live there.

至于北极,众所周知,它不仅是个能<u>冻死</u>人的地方,而且像你我之辈是不可能在那儿生活下来的。 （副词＋形容词→动词＋动词）

◇ In practice, this is <u>an advantage</u> to the aeroplane, which is already at a <u>good</u> height when it reaches the polar region.

实际上这对飞机来说是极为<u>有利</u>的,因为当飞机进入极地时已经飞得<u>相当高</u>了。 （名词→形容词,形容词→副词）

◇ Another scientist asserts that direct mind-<u>to</u>-mind communication will replace phone calls and faxes.

另一位科学家断言思想<u>与</u>思想的直接交流将取代电话和传真。

（介词→连词）

◇ Their job was to compile data on any errors in key systems <u>across</u> the U. S.

他们的任务是为<u>全</u>美主要系统编制障碍数据。 （介词→形容词）

══════ 练　　习 ══════

1．翻译短文：

China is the third largest country in the world, and its vast area includes the extremes of climate, vegetation, topography and population. The span of recorded Chinese history covers 4000 years and this was preceded by a prehistoric era of 600,000 years. Archaeologists are making new discoveries all the time. The figure usually quoted for China's population is 1.2 billion. The ethnic fabric of China consists of 94 per cent Han people and 6 per cent national minorities who live in the border areas. The founding of the People's Republic in 1949 marked a new phase in Chinese history.

2．完成下列句子的翻译：

(1) We can make a cake with the flour, milk and eggs that we have bought.

我们可以用＿＿＿＿＿＿＿＿＿＿＿＿＿＿＿＿＿＿做一个蛋糕。

(2) There was a lot of damage to both cars, and both John and the other man were hurt.

＿＿＿＿＿＿＿＿＿＿＿＿＿＿＿＿＿＿约翰和另一个人都受了伤。

(3) Five days in the week, she goes to King's Cross station in London by train, then she gets in a bus and goes to her office in Holborn.

她每周五天从伦敦的国王十字车站坐火车＿＿＿＿＿＿＿＿＿＿＿＿。

(4) Like many bachelors approaching middle age, he was getting rather set in his ways.

像许多进入中年的单身汉一样_____。

(5) People who live on the slopes of an active volcano know that at any moment every-thing they possess may be swept away by molten lava.

居住在活火山山坡上的人都知道_____。

(6) Olympic Games of 1900 and 1904 were tied up with business, because they were organised as a secondary attraction to international trade fairs.

1900 年 和 1904 年 的 奥 林 匹 克 运 动 会 跟 做 生 意 结 合，_____

_____。

(7) He walked up to the front door and opened it quietly. He listened carefully for a few moments but could hear nothing.

他走到大门,悄悄地把它打开,_____。

3. 用词类转换法翻译下列句子：

(1) I owe a very special word of thanks to you for your help.

(2) Computers have found wide application for our daily work.

(3) He's traveled all over the world. Up the Rhine. Across the Pyrenees. To the United States. Over the Pacific.

(4) Familiarity doesn't always symbolize friendship.

(5) His father doesn't wish to see him physically strong but mentally weak.

(6) There is a close agreement between the school and the company upon the installa-tion of computers in the office.

(7) We are grateful to you for your unfailing support.

Lesson 31
Shared Thoughts and Values

What is culture? It is generally defined as knowledge, beliefs and thoughts shared by members of a community. People use cultural knowledge to understand each other's experience and to guide their daily behaviour. When people share a culture, this means that they have a shared language and communication style as well as shared customs, attitudes and values.①

When we are in a new culture or meet someone from a different culture, we see that people greet one another, give compliments and respond to them in different ways. In China it is appropriate for students to call their teachers "Laoshi (teacher)", but few American professors think it is rude if their students call them by their first name. When a colleague gives compliments such as "The party is wonderful", "Your girl friend is beautiful", "You've made a good speech", "Your house is really nice" or "Your Chinese is excellent", Europeans are likely to accept them by saying "Thank you." But a Chinese may disagree with or even deny such a compliment, because he or she thinks it important to take a modest attitude towards complimentary remarks.②

In many Asian cultures people feel that they stand on ceremony if they give compliments to their parents, husband, wife or close friends. They can be very grateful to their family members for their help, but they may not verbalize their thanks.

A group of Hong Kong students gave a *hongbao* (gift money in a red envelope) to their American professor for his good tuition. To their surprise he appreciated their gift but was confused and felt very bad about it.③

When one is exposed to another culture, one finds it difficult to express one's ideas and feelings. It is possible that people miscommunicate with each other even in their own culture. When they are sad, sick, in a hurry or fed up with somebody, they may say something with an implied meaning and leave it for the listeners to figure out.

In some culture it is okay if one says "No, you are wrong" when correcting somebody. But many English speakers may say, "Well, I think you may be wrong," or "If I were you I would have done it in another way."

Wherever you are, you are not supposed to ask a lady about her age, or a man about his salaries, or a Muslim cook about pork dishes even if it is acceptable to do so in your country. ④

It is understandable that foreign students may make phonetic, grammar or semantic mistakes when they speak or write Chinese. However it would be better if they try to avoid the expressions that they don't understand exactly. The native speakers are sensitive about the words or expressions whose meaning is ambiguous.

Human beings are the culture-bearing animals. Language is a carrier of culture⑤with which they are able to communicate with one another, inherit the past, understand the present and plan the future. If a language link is broken the communicators will lose the culture that they share.

● 注　　释 ●

① When people share a culture, this means…as well as shared customs, attitudes and values.

有共同的文化就意味着……以及共同的风俗、共同的态度和价值观念。

② because he or she thinks it is important to take a modest attitude towards complimentary remarks.

因为他或她觉得重要的是对于赞扬的话应该持谦虚的态度。

③ To their surprise he appreciated their gift but was confused and felt very bad about it.

令人奇怪的是：老师虽然感谢他们送的红包，但是很不理解，感到不愉快。

④ you are not supposed to ask a lady about her age, or a man about his salaries, or a Muslim cook about pork dishes even if it is acceptable to do so in your country.

你不应该问女士的年龄，问男士的工资，问穆斯林厨师有关猪肉的菜肴的问题。即便在自己国家可以问在其他国家也不行。

⑤ Language is a carrier of culture

语言是文化的载体

※ 译法分析 ※

翻译中词量的对应问题

把一个英语短句译为汉语时两者的词量可能对应，如：

◇ Are you web surfers or online chatters?

你是网上冲浪者还是网上侃爷？

◇ The major religions in China are Taoism, Buddhism, Islam and Christianity.

中国的主要宗教有:道教、佛教、伊斯兰教和基督教。

◇ People use cultural knowledge to understand each other's experience and to guide their daily behaviour.

人们用文化知识了解彼此的经验并指导自己的日常活动。

但是这样的例子并不很多。在成段、成篇、成部的翻译中,原文和译文绝大部分在词量、词性、语序和句法结构方面是不必要也不可能逐字逐句对应的。如:

◇ We all know that it is possible for ordinary people to make their homes on the equator, although often they feel uncomfortably hot there.

我们都知道,虽然普通人在赤道地区往往会感到炎热难当,但是在那儿安家还是可能的。

◇ After 35 years we had to move out of our house. How does one say good-bye to a house?

我们要搬出住了 35 年的旧居,如何舍得离开?

◇ They claim that their product, Protena, tastes, smells and looks just like meat.

他们声称他们的产品普罗特纳色、香、味都和肉一样。

有些学生把汉语的"大象"译为"great elephant",把"小孩"译为"little child",把"老师"译为"old teacher",显然这样的翻译包含着冗余成分,因为"elephant"、"child"、"teacher"就是那三个汉语词语的英语对应形式。

 练　习

1. 翻译短文:

Lately I've begun to think that many of my favourite sayings are simply out of date. That realization hit home while I was stooping to retrieve a coin. "A penny saved is a penny earned," I said. My teenage daughter frowned. "What does that mean? You can't buy anything with a penny," she stated in a matter-of-fact way. "You're missing the point," I protested. But was she? Or was I? Consider the time-honoured phrase "killing two birds with one stone." The last time I said that, my young naturalist neighbour was aghast. "You're not actually destroying our feathered wildlife!" he exclaimed, and stalked off.

2. 翻译下列句子:

(1) Regards from us all. Our best wishes to David. Say hello to Ann for me. Looking forward to hearing from you.

(2) Choose the word or phrase from the alternative given which is closest in meaning to the words in italics in the context of the passage.

(3) They may not come at all. They may never have intended to turn up. They may be sitting in a pub having a drink.

(4) First Peter couldn't start the car. Then we had to stop at the garage for some petrol. Then we couldn't find anywhere to park but in the end we were able to squeeze into a gap just round the corner.

(5) Everything in the safe was gone. About three hundred pounds in notes, some premium bonds and most important, my stamp collection, which must be worth at least ten thousand pounds.

(6) A good guide to what is psychologically healthy for a small child is therefore provided by a television series in which a boy and girl are supposed to be exploring distant planets with their parents.

(7) It's no use looking at me! You know what I'm like. I can't tell left from right. But I can't imagine why you didn't look up the route before we set out.

3. 翻译下面的歌词:

Winter Wonderland

Over the ground lies a mantle of white,

A heaven of diamonds shines down through the night,

Two hearts are thrilling in spite of the chill in the weather.

Love knows no seasons, love knows no clime,

Romance can blossom any old time.

Here in the open we're walking and hoping together,

Sleigh bells ring — are you listening?

In the lane, snow is glistening,

A beautiful sight, we're happy tonight, walkin' in a winter wonderland.

Lesson 32
Language and Culture

　　使用不同语言的民族,历史渊源、地理环境、社会现状、政治制度、道德风尚均不相同,人们的价值观念、思维逻辑、生活方式、审美情趣也不一样。作为社会产物和文化载体的语言,自然无处不体现所属民族的文化。一个译者尽管较好地掌握了所译语言的语音、词汇、语法和修辞知识,但是如果对原文所体现的社会文化缺乏充分的了解,就不能把握所译文字的思想实质和深刻含义,就不能把它准确地转达出来。

　　语言中的文化因素隐含在语言的多个方面,语言之间的文化差异有时是微妙的。原文中的每一个词语、句子、段落和篇章都提供了或多或少的文化信息,译者的责任就是要把它连同原文的词汇和语法意义尽可能完整地传递给读者。

　　文化意义隐含在词汇方面。中国是一个历史悠久的国家,人口众多,地大物博,封建统治长达 2000 多年,农业经济长期占主导地位,与外国文化经济交流密切。这些特点在汉语词汇方面的体现是:文化艺术词汇、农业词汇、外来语词汇都很丰富。英语国家情况不尽相同,但是受英国传统文化和欧美文化影响较深,经济发达,现代科学技术处于领先地位。反映到英语词汇中,航海和科技词汇丰富,新词不断涌现,外语借词很多。译者如果了解中国和英语国家的历史和社会情况,对于两种语言的理解就会更加深刻,翻译就会更加准确。

　　民族文化直接影响思维和表达方式。汉语和英语在构词、造句和叙述中,对于人神、主宾、官民、男女、尊卑、上下、左右、前后、今昔、因果、大小、强弱、好劣等对立的范畴、等级和概念都有自己的表达顺序。中国人常使用由大到小、先主后宾、由远及近、先男后女、从左到右、先一般后个别、先假设后推理、先概括后分述的表达模式。这些模式有许多跟对应的英语方式相反或者不完全一致。例如汉语年月日和地址的表达顺序是由大到小,而英语则刚好相反;汉语的条件句和假设句中主句和分句的次序在大多数情况下是强制性的,而英语的同类句式则是选择性的。

　　汉语和英语都有它的简约性。但是英语的简约性主要表现在形态变化的简化、缩略语和紧缩形式的使用以及非正式表达中词语最大限度的省略。而汉语许多词语同时具有单音节和双音节形式,使用大量流水句,具有多种省略方式,如:承前省、蒙后省、承宾省、承定省等等,这些特点英语是无法比拟的。

　　汉语和英语的许多成语和固定词组往往隐含着浓厚的民族文化积淀,仅从文字表面的含义来理解是不够的,有时还可能产生误解。例如汉语的"长城"、

"借东风"、"狐狸精"、"赛诸葛"、"活雷锋"、"上方宝剑"、"铁人精神"、"武松打虎",英语的"B & B"、"motel"、"hippy"、"bingo"、"sandwich man"、"bushwalking"、"Send him to Newcastle"、"Mud in your eye"等。这些词语一般都不容易直译,翻译时须认真推敲。

◎ 思 考 题 ◎

1. 语言与文化之间有什么关系?请举例说明。
2. 语言中的文化因素主要体现在哪些方面?请举例说明。
3. 民族文化对思维方式的影响主要表现在哪些方面?
4. 民族文化对语言表达的影响主要表现在哪些方面?
5. 汉语和英语的简约性有哪些异同?
6. 语言中的文化因素对翻译有什么影响?

Appendix

有关翻译理论与技巧的参考书目

张培基、喻云根等,1980。《英汉翻译教程》,上海:上海外语教育出版社。

刘靖之(编),1981。《翻译论集》,香港:生活·读书·新知三联书店。

张 今,1981。《英汉比较语法纲要》,北京:商务印书馆。

吴洁敏,1982。《汉英语法比较》,北京:知识出版社。

肖君石,1982。《汉英、英汉翻译初探》,北京:商务印书馆。

陈胥华,1984。《英汉对译指导》,武汉:湖北教育出版社。

刘宓庆,1985。《文体与翻译》,北京:中国对外翻译出版公司。

黄龙,1986。《翻译技巧指导》,沈阳:辽宁人民出版社。

《中国翻译》编辑部(编),1986。《论英汉翻译技巧》,北京:中国对外翻译出版公司。

邓炎昌、刘润清,1989。《语言与文化》,北京:外语教学与研究出版社。

王 还,1993。《汉英对比论文集》,北京:北京语言学院出版社。

熊文华,1997。《汉英应用对比概论》,北京:北京语言文化大学出版社。

刘重德(编),1998。《英汉比较与翻译》,青岛:青岛出版社。

萧立明(编),1998。《英汉语比较研究》,长沙:湖南人民出版社。